LIVING SPIRITUALITY

LIVING SPIRITUALITY

ILLUMINATING THE PATH

Gregory J. Laughery

Destinée S.A.
Huémoz, Switzerland

Published by Destinée S.A., www.destinee.ch
Book formatting by Deborah Meacham and Jasie Peltier
Cover design by Alex Grudem and Sarah Grasmick
Copy editing by Kathleen Hanson
All rights reserved by the author.

ISBN 978-0-9759082-5-9

CONTENTS

Part Four: The End of the Journey: A New Beginning

Acknowledgements

I wish to express my gratitude to all the people that I have had the privilege to live with and learn from over the many years of being associated with the L'Abri Fellowship in Switzerland. Living in this thriving and active community has provided the context for work, study, scholarship, reflection, and intensive discussion with a myriad of people. The richness, uniqueness, and opportunity of being part of a Christian community are indeed merciful and redemptive.

Special thanks go to my wife Elizabeth, and our children: Vincent, Alexander and Lawrence. All of you encourage and support me in many ways. Each family member is a loving and challenging partner in conversation, and together a cherished community.

I am also deeply grateful for a group of beloved friends. George and Eileen Diepstra, in particular, have shared the journey for the last twenty-five years. They devoted precious time out of their busy schedules to read and comment on drafts of this book, and it is no doubt better because of their gracious efforts.

In addition, Anna Elkins spent months working through this text. She took it apart and put it together, and its present state owes much to her skills. Merci Anna.

Francis and Edith Schaeffer, the founders of L'Abri, both wrote influential books on Christian spirituality. I am indebted to them and thankful for their writings. They were and continue to be an important stimulus to my own work, as I explore and discover the dynamics of a biblical understanding of living spirituality.

Preface

L'Abri, the French word for shelter, is a spiritual shelter for anyone in need of spiritual help. Literally thousands have studied here, taken part in this community, and had their lives changed. Significant numbers of people continue to stream into Swiss L'Abri and other branches. Many come seeking answers to the modern/postmodern questions and dilemmas of today. Others are searching for a deeper faith in Christ or grappling with inner strife. Still others are bewildered about spirituality. Those who study with us have the opportunity to work through diverse struggles and to address serious issues that demand careful consideration. Together we hammer out true and applicable responses for living a Christian life individually, in community, and in the world.

Recently, Swiss L'Abri celebrated its fiftieth anniversary. Indeed, quite a remarkable duration for a Christian community. Several things contribute to this ongoing longevity including: the faithfulness of God, prayer, generous unsolicited donations (viewed by us who live here as responses to prayer), giving honest answers to honest questions, and attempting to demonstrate something of the reality of the existence of God for the whole of life.

Central to the heartbeat of Christianity and to L'Abri is the reality of community with God and his people, a focus on the Bible as true truth, the redemptive work of Christ in the power of the Spirit, and cultivating both a living and true spirituality. These vital realities present a constant and worthy challenge for life together.

The material for the book you have in your hands has developed during my time of working at Swiss L'Abri. If I were to add up all the hours, I have probably spent years in discussion with international students and working adults. Sharing their valid concerns, genuine questions, and deep perplexities about Christian spirituality challenged me to work through my own views and to pursue legitimate responses, which you now have before you in these pages.

In today's climate of escalating ambiguity and spiritual impoverishment in our own circles, I believe that Christians acutely need living spirituality. This book aims to help us discover and recover a profound sense of Christian spirituality, and the reality it points us to. And then to live it in real and credible ways. Yet, what is it that we are to live? What path are we to take that will lead us to life?

Part One
Spirituality in our Times

1

The Landscape

Spirituality is an exceedingly captivating topic, and of enormous interest today, although our recent past shows that this was not always the case. Threatened by a thriving twentieth-century naturalism, bolstered by the rising force of a scientific worldview, spirituality looked like it might disappear. A coercive secularization of culture and church was also well underway, and it seemed as if this powerful alliance would extinguish the pursuit of a spiritual life and experience.

Yet, stunningly, the opposite is taking place and spirituality is flourishing. In the twilight of the twentieth-century, and early in the twenty-first, there is an extraordinary attraction to spirituality. This prevalence is clearly visible in North America and Europe, but also evident in other regions of the planet. Intrigued by the mysteries, uncertainties, and perplexities of life, the quest for spirituality enchants us. We passionately search for that which is within or beyond to help us explain the world, but so often get confused and are unsure of the way forward.

Think of the popularity of films like *The Lord of the Rings, The Matrix,* and *The Passion;* books like Rick Warren's, *The Purpose*

Driven Life and Thomas Moore's, *Care of the Soul*; TV shows like Oprah; the music of Nick Cave, Sting, and U2. They all express one spiritual focus or another. These media, and their phenomenal success, are piercing echoes of our current interest in spirituality. And it is a seemingly unquenchable interest. Clearly, a fascination with spirituality is now everywhere. While a pursuit of the spiritual may be positive, I wonder where all this fervor leaves us.

Into the Ambiguous

My view on this is that in spite of the enchantment with spirituality in our times, the perplexity of the subject remains daunting. Significant questions arise. What is spirituality? And how is it to be cultivated and lived today?

To heighten the importance of responding to these questions just reflect for a moment. We now live in a culture where proliferations of spiritualities are circulating in a wide diversity of expressions. There is no lack of spiritual options for us. Our world is clogged with a concoction of new age, kitsch, neo-pagan, as well as cultural, non-Christian, and Christian persuasions. We're offered the realms of *shuffle* and *shopping* spirituality. Anything goes. Just mix it all together and hope for the best. What are we to make of all this, and where is it leading us?

One of my main interests in writing this book is to address the escalating forms of ambiguity in the "shuffle" and "shopping" spirituality of our times and to offer a Christian response. I do so particularly for Christian readers, but also for those who struggle with a sense of being adrift in the sea of spiritualities currently available.

Increasing ambiguity is reigning. As I see it, the spiritual predicament confronting Christians today presents a two-fold challenge: the rising attraction to cultural and non-Christian forms of spirituality on the one hand, and the impoverishment of Christian spirituality on the other.

To begin I'd like to sketch out the first challenge and its contribution to ambiguity: the growing allure of cultural and non-Christian forms of spirituality. In the context of our enhanced awareness and updated interest in the search for spirituality some say that a spiritual revolution is taking place. One manifestation goes something like this—being *spiritual* is whatever you make it to be. You buy into the marketing strategies of the random, of surpassing the mundane, and of reveling in fragmentation. You have come to believe that if you just turn up the volume on your iPod or stereo and hit "shuffle" the music will transport you into the world of your reveries.

This supposedly safe or enriching spiritual space is just one of many mistaken for living spirituality. While searching for the soundtrack to your life, you don't truly listen to the words being sung to you. This easy and free approach of "shuffle spirituality" reinforces the contemporary mindset of a *make it up as you go along* spirituality, but lacks any real power to transform lives.

Another manifestation that many adhere to views the search for spirituality as an exercise in comparison shopping to find just the right style of religion or spirituality for you. A friend recently shared an example of this with me. It came in the form of a cardboard wheel with an arrow that one could spin around and in so doing view the offer of thirty religious options.

The marketing technique was, "choose your own religion: a search engine for life." The label acknowledged the significance of spirituality yet touted any religious persuasion or combination of them as an equally valid way to the spiritual. The less direct message was: compare and shop for whatever religious orientation suits you. This guide to religion attempts to banish your anxiety by animating fashionable "shopping spirituality," but it falls far short of any authentic capacity to regenerate lives.

In addition to "shuffle" and "shopping" spirituality there are further examples of our spiritually ambiguous times everywhere; such as fundamentalist terrorism, dwindling church attendance, polarized religious relativism or dogmatism, the stunning popularity of kitsch portrayed by religious trinkets propped up on one's desk or dashboard, and various formulations of a thriving postmodern religion without a transcendent-redemptive God. The times are mystifying. Each of these trends tells part of the confusing spiritual story of our age. In the midst of the driving enthusiasm and obsessive quest for a spiritual life, *spirituality* has come to mean everything, yet nothing.

As Christians, what are we to make of this? Should the spirituality frenzy today be viewed positively, negatively, or simply ignored? Do we just go with the flow, trusting that whatever is trendy is spiritual? Are we to simply embrace any one of the plethora of cultural or religious forms and modes of spirituality without thinking about it? My concern is that we lack an informed response to these types of questions.

Invitation to Grace and New Life

Before turning to the second challenge, the impoverishment of Christian spirituality, I think it is important to tell you where I'm coming from. Why? As the author of this book, I believe that you should know where I stand and kneel as one who has received the Infinite One's offer of grace, redemption, and community. And I want you to see the broader application of this as it relates to the search for spirituality.

I wish to make two key perspectives clear. First, the "living" in *living spirituality*, as I am using it, is both verb and adjective. That is, this spirituality is to "be lived" and it is a spirituality that "is living." Second, it is my view that to make contact with the source of this spirituality, to come into a living and dynamic community with the One who makes spirituality happen, it is essential to be a Christian. The Bible teaches us that in order to be living spirituality in our present context, we must first be disciples of Jesus.

4

This, of course, may appear obvious. Yet in our Western and broadly ambiguous and spiritually relativistic cultural context, there is an urgency to think again. A vast spectrum of people have some notion of spirituality, although they are not necessarily followers of the Lord Jesus Christ, while others who may acknowledge Christ, seek to incorporate diverse cultural or non-Christian forms of spirituality into their lives. If all paths lead to spirituality, then why bother with distinctions?

Living spirituality without distinction, however, is an illusion. It is important to underline this. From a Christian perspective conversion to Christ is *the* only gateway to a truly spiritual life. In order to illustrate this access into true community with God, and to highlight living spirituality as a distinct spirituality, I want to give you two real life examples that reflect two characters portrayed in John's gospel.

Jerry's story

Jerry came into my office for another tutorial. He had been at L'Abri for several months deeply wrestling with serious questions and issues. As a God-fearing man from a Jewish family, Jerry had a meticulous view of keeping rules, codes and regimes that he embraced as spiritual. During his time in the community here, some of this understanding began to crumble, bringing to light crucial questions about life, death, and spirituality. In our tutorial we discussed many significant ideas and struggles relating to these issues. "Greg," he asked finally, "what is life all about? I have heard of Jesus, but how does he have anything to do with it?"

For a start, I told him, Jesus is the Messiah, the savior of Israel and the world. He taught many radical and innovative things. One of the most important was that he can release you from sin, which separates you from God. Being born anew, to be born of water and Spirit are necessary if you are to enter into community with God and to be living spirituality. So it is: Flesh produces flesh, but the

Spirit gives birth to spirit. It all begins here. Jerry listened carefully and took this away with him that day.

Sheila's story

Sheila shared some of the same concerns as Jerry, but came from a different background and situation. She was brought up in a Christian family, was divorced, and was involved with a man who was not her husband. In her social context, many viewed her as an outcast, and she had come here seeking shelter and refuge.

The time in the community challenged her to reflect on truth and the path to spiritual rejuvenation of moving from death to life. One day I was out for a walk, and I passed her on the village road. She stopped to ask me a question. In puzzled dismay, Sheila wondered if she could be a spiritual person. She had been battling with the question for months. "What does Jesus have to do with life and death?" she asked. We sat on a bench nearby and talked it over.

Following an intense discussion on the dynamics of life and death, moral culpability before God, grace, and the need for redemption, I mentioned that Jesus is the one who offers her living water. The promise to her, and to anyone who drinks this water, is that they will never be thirsty. It is the water of everlasting life that gives you community with God, ushers you into living spirituality, and quenches your thirst forever. She went on to learn a lesson that we all must learn: God is spirit, and everyone—regardless of race or creed—is to worship him in spirit and truth.

These two real life scenarios, with the answers given modeled on Jesus' teaching to Nicodemus and the Samaritan woman, point us to the only way into community with God and living spirituality. Jesus is the gateway. Everyone is invited. Neither Jesus, nor the Spirit imposes a selective guest list. Whether we are like Jerry or Sheila, or from an entirely different situation or place, we are offered superabundant grace through Jesus Christ and the agency of the Spirit.

When it is understood that Jesus Christ is the gateway to living spirituality, significant opportunities open up for us: to be in community with the Infinite-personal God, to taste living water, and to experience a new birth of the Spirit through faith in the crucified and risen One. When we accept the invitation to walk through the gateway, our world *explodes* because we confess that it's no longer centered on ourselves or all about us. And it is then that we start to find our place in living spirituality and to discover the true meaning of life in all its richness and mystery.

Living and true spirituality therefore is deeply rooted in following Jesus. Walking through the gateway is essential. To follow the crucified and risen One is not a matter of giving a performance, reciting a mantra, or having a religious inclination or feeling. First and foremost, it is a matter of the whole person acknowledging and then bowing before the God who is there, accepting Christ as Lord and Savior, and receiving the gift of the Spirit.

This is the beginning of a life-long journey—a task and a joy. But it is merely the beginning. The true spiritual life is not less than stepping through the gateway, but inevitably much, much more as we will see later.

Spiritual Impoverishment and Adding to the Ambiguity

After understanding the importance of following Jesus and receiving new life to be living spirituality, we are now going to face the second challenge: impoverished Christian spirituality and its contribution to increased ambiguity.

Impoverishment takes many forms and may be expressed in several ways. Christians, perhaps unwittingly, often contribute to the spirituality chaos of our times, instead of helping to diminish it. We fuel the flames of unacceptable degrees of ambiguity. How? One of the major, if not-so-obvious ways we contribute is through our tendency to succumb to false, but powerful *absolutizing* forces that may approach us or even reside in us. Some, for example, assume that Christian spirituality is absolutely anchored in reason, seeing, feeling, or experience. This type of absolutizing may seem to counter ambiguity, but it actually increases it by attempting to encapsulate spirituality in a one-dimensional manner and to do away with a necessary dialogical tension, which I will say more about later.

For now, let's take a closer look at one of the most prominent examples of false absolutizing in today's context: feeling. Numerous Christians have informed me that spirituality is what they feel. If that is the case, as they believe, then it can be spiritual to break vows and commitments when feeling depressed, to ignore a job contract when feeling overworked, to take a vacation instead of paying bills when feeling spring fever, or to divorce one's husband or wife when feeling unloved. The danger of such a highly subjective perspective is that it dupes us and others to buy into a warped notion of Christian spirituality.

Within "feeling" Christian circles, the concept of spirituality becomes highly mystifying. It turns into feeling without content, which then becomes absolute and unquestionable. It also happens, often unwittingly, to become the same as anyone else's spirituality and therefore contributes to ambiguity. Do these sound familiar?

If you feel it, it's spiritual.

If you feel it, it must be true.

Don't get me wrong, feelings are a wonderful part of being human, and they do have a key place in living spirituality. But there is a problem if absolutized feelings reign. If we merely equate feelings with truth and spirituality, how do we ever critique them?

When it comes to spirituality these days, a critical perspective is frequently missing. Such a critique is unlikely in today's environment, because we are driven—even consumed by—feeling. Our lives are dominated by how we feel, what we feel, and when we feel it. In this context, our feelings become absolutized and function as the sole determiner of what constitutes spirituality. Operating with this kind of blind trust in feelings, we fail to recognize their potential deficiency for determining what is true or spiritual, and this leaves us wide open for self-deception.

Again, I am not saying that we can or should ignore our feelings. They can often be indicators of a deep longing for love, accurate suspicion, and the quest for hope. But neither should we be enslaved to feelings, because they can also deceive us. Therefore, it is important to be able to check them for trustworthiness. To do so we need to be in a personal and community *dialogue* with God, the crucified and risen Christ, the Spirit, the biblical text, other people in community, and the world in which we live. These dialogue partners will lead us into a deeper contemplation of what is truly spiritual.

Sound complicated? Well, it is. To begin to reverse the flow of spiritual impoverishment and to diminish ambiguity, it is essential to realize that the scope of living spirituality is a complex and dynamic matter that requires us to take into consideration more than the way we *feel*. To *feel* that this or that is spiritual is a feeling. On its own, it is unable to help us navigate our way through to a living spirituality, which is dependent on far more than the way we feel.

In addition to feelings and the dialogue partners mentioned above, I also want to include rationality, sense observation, experience, and imagination as having a role in living spirituality. Yet when feelings or any of these other perspectives reign absolute, we risk losing any potential for critical distance, and we exclude dialogue, which means that our interaction with other partners and orientations borders on irrelevance or worse, non-existence.

This leads us to several questions: How should followers of Jesus evaluate spirituality? Do we have cause for queries? Is our spirituality really true and living? To start answering these questions and to further work our way towards diminishing ambiguity and reversing spiritual impoverishment, let's briefly chart out some of the dynamics for living spirituality that are important to have in place.

2

Living Spirituality and the Way Ahead

In spite of an impoverished spirituality and accelerating ambiguity, there is a true and living spirituality for those who follow in the footsteps of the crucified and risen One. As we proceed, remember that I am using the "living" in *living spirituality* as both verb and adjective.

I now want to highlight three basic dimensions of this spirituality that are woven into the fabric of this book. In the rest of this chapter, I wish to discuss the spiritual dynamics of life and death, to offer an explanation as to why our spirituality is impoverished, and then to suggest ways to reverse this by embracing living spirituality.

It is holistic
Living spirituality is a holistic project of affirming life over death. That is, its concerns are diverse and its dialogues many. It goes beyond closed-minded exclusivism that sees spirituality as merely a *religious* matter that is unrelated to the arts, ecology, music, politics, and all facets of life.

It is interactive

Living spirituality explores the interaction between humans and the Spirit of God—with both receiving adequate attention. It is centered on theology, not merely anthropology, psychology, or sociology; although each of these are valid considerations concerning the spiritual life. It applies to being and becoming holy; to discovering the truth of God in relation and distinction and all this means; to integrating biblical ideas and culture where possible; and to the necessity of going beyond ourselves—transcending self and finding a new self in recognition of the God who has graciously revealed himself.

It is interpretative

This spirituality includes an interpretative dimension encompassing the whole of life. By this I mean that it is connected to interpreting normal human understanding and explaining it through the interpretation of the Bible, which leads to new understanding. In other words, there is a necessary movement from interpreting our life in the world, to a critical analysis of it, and then to a transformation—through the Spirit into the image of Christ.

We will look at other basic dimensions later, but for now these three give us a start in understanding living spirituality. Ignoring any of these basics is an invitation to higher levels of ambiguity and spiritual impoverishment, which eventually opens up the more weighty issues of *life* and *death*. That is to say, decreasing ambiguity and reversing spiritual impoverishment are vital to our own spirituality. The goal here that should touch everything else is to be a renewed life in Christ, empowered by the Spirit, in community with the God who is there, others, and the world: living spirituality. Keep the relevance of this goal, and the basic dimensions in mind as we continue.

Staying Alert: Life and death

Faced with the proliferation of cultural and non-Christian forms of spirituality, new idolatries, kitsch, and *khora* (that all-consuming emptiness that some postmodern practitioners prefer to the God of Scripture), we have an urgent need to be vigilant against that which is dying. Many of these spiritualities and others veer toward destruction. That may sound harsh, but any spirituality that denies true community with the God of the Bible leads to death. *Consider this and contemplate it carefully.*

If we are going to begin to live a less impoverished spirituality it is crucial to be attentive. Living spirituality gives us a sacred mandate to be acutely aware of orientations to life or to death. God is for life. And that matters for us now. From a biblical perspective, spiritual life and death are not some far-off and merely future concerns. They also refer to the present and the importance of how we live in it. The massive and ultimate question is: what shall we choose today—life or death? *What is your choice? Assess it thoughtfully.*

The gospel of John consistently maintains that Jesus Christ is the way, the truth, and the life (14:6-7). He was the true light that shattered darkness and brought life into the world.

Several verses in John explain this: "In him was life, and the life was the light of all people. The light shines in the darkness and the darkness did not overcome it" (1:4-5 NRSV). Christ said, "I am the light of the world. Whoever follows me will never walk in darkness, but will have the light of life" (8:12). *Meditate reflectively on these words.*

Following Christ is to live—to live in the light so that our present lives are a sign of his love and commandments. In the face of death and dying spiritualities we are called to embrace this life now.

Appearances

What does this look like? Unfortunately, many Christians are perplexed. Is it a personal peace, a fully spiritual existence, a carefree life, a deep feeling or experience of oneness with all that exists? In my view, it is none of these.

I have discussed this question with a variety of believers over the past twenty-five years, and they have consistently responded in an obscure manner, which leads me to a lamentable conclusion: high levels of ambiguity and spiritual impoverishment foster a growing inability to capture and be captured by living spirituality, to live it individually, in community, and out into the world. Entrapped in feeble understanding and insufficient explanation, there is little or no new understanding of what living and true spirituality looks like.

Regrettably, expressions of cultural and non-Christian forms of spirituality (dying spiritualities because they are not aligned with the God who lives) all too often influence, entice, and appear more plausible to us. Why is Christian spirituality so impoverished that we are lured into the dying? There are several reasons for this unfortunate situation in our times, but I want to alert you to two in particular.

Lack of education

First, I believe that in many contemporary Christian contexts, there is a lamentable lack of teaching on biblical spirituality. Insufficient effort is put into educating and equipping Christians to carefully read, contemplate, and internalize Scripture, to be in touch with and transformed by the Spirit, to engage the world of ideas, and to evaluate the driving forces behind cultural and non-Christian forms of spirituality.

A failure to educate and equip followers of Christ has corrosive effects. We tend to latch onto whatever is trendy without giving it careful consideration. We seem unable to be captivated by the Bible, to grapple seriously with ideas, or to comprehend the radical

14

difference between living spirituality and other spiritualities. And we get confused about the only true way towards life. These types of debilitating consequences result in a lack of wisdom, and a growing inability to grasp the importance of being well informed about our spirituality and worldview.

Institutionalization of churches

Second, a myriad of churches have gone the way of the institution. The word "Christian" has taken on an institutional or religious definition characterized by an indifference that seems far from engaging with people and their real needs and problems. This is partially due to the fact that Christians often seem to be primarily interested in themselves: propagating their programs, building their churches, even manipulating some of their own in order to achieve social status and accomplish their goals and aims. People are left behind in the wake of promising words that give the pretense of care and concern, but translate into intolerable levels of neglect and inconsistent waffling.

As a result of what is too often the large gap between words and actions, some have become extremely suspicious of whether there is even a link between the words *Christian* and *spirituality*. In engaging with those who call themselves Christians, they observe hollow and superficial ideologies and practical lives that fail to reflect the face of Christ. A lamentable lack of the reality of love, of authenticity, and the "real" become reasons for avoiding all things and people labeled *Christian*. This skeptical and increasingly cynical audience still seeks after spirituality, but it begins to abandon any conception of the compatibility of *Christian* and *spirituality*.

The more a church functions as an institution preaching its own survival, the less opportunity there is for people to hear the gospel, to experience community life, or to find a loving spiritual home. Entertainment may be there, and the double negative: *all* or *none* of the answers to life's important questions could be there, but the reality of holistic, interactive, and interpretative living spirituality is acutely absent. Cold, mechanical, forced religiosity or warm, fuzzy, superficiality will rightly bring forth suspicion, apathy, and rejection by those who have valid concerns about what is authentic and true.

Even as Christians today desperately strive for the authentic, they have never been so captured by that which is inauthentic. Thwarted by "shopping" and "shuffle" spirituality, cultural materialism, and the syrupy sweetness of comfortable idealism, living spirituality becomes a mirage and Christian credibility wanes.

What does living spirituality look like? As I have pointed out in the previous pages, many churches and Christians are lacking vision. To counter this, we now need to trace out an answer to this question by doing some serious reflection on helpful ways to reverse our spiritual impoverishment and our attractions to the dying. Let's move in new directions that will enliven the spirituality we are to live.

The Reversal: Saying, Doing, Educating, Loving

There are several key ways to reverse spiritual impoverishment in our lives in general, and in our churches in particular. For now, I want to highlight two. First, we must make an effort to embody the biblical mandate of living a greater consistency between our words and actions. Conversion to Christ, the power of redemption, and the personal agency of the Spirit unlock the door for this to begin to take place, but it is imperative to live it in refreshing and life-giving ways. That is to say, who we are, what we say, and what we do are all relevant to living spirituality, a life lived before God, ourselves, and others.

Authenticity is essential. For a start, we need to be real—to be vulnerable, even sacrificial. We need to be every-day people living in the real world. To both stand for and live the truth in love. We want to be a testimony and demonstration that we love each other and all people. If we expect Christian spirituality to flourish in the world and to better understand it for our own lives, we have to look to the Spirit and translate the crucified and risen One's words of love, hope, compassion, honesty, and integrity into actions. This looking and translating is living spirituality. Of course, the translation is never perfect, and at times it will break down. Still, as we live in God's world, there is to be a continual attempt to demonstrate a transformed life for the sake of—and to the glory of—God.

Sadly, Christians far too often fail to express love to those both inside and outside of the Christian community. There is too much talk and too little action. Through renewal we will be able to show Christ's love to each other and our neighbors. The beauty of active Christian love is compelling, and it helps others to acknowledge that God is with us.

Second, Christians and churches have a responsibility for pointing the way forward. We are responsible for relevant biblical teaching on spirituality and a host of other topics; for educating and equipping believers to live as salt and light in the world; for illuminating the path ahead through creating loving communities that listen, that both nourish their members in the truth and invite a real sense of participation amongst them.

People are looking for community, credibility, and authenticity—not merely an institutional program. Far too often, Christians are starving for love and personal involvement which goes unfulfilled. And then there are numerous believers and others who need someone to be in dialogue with them concerning their reasons for shunning active involvement in church.

Biblical spirituality desperately needs to be taught and lived in deep, loving, cutting-edge ways within both the church context and the whole of life if we are going to begin to reverse impoverishment and the allure of the dying. To do so is to promote a more robust and well informed spirituality that is capable of being authentically lived individually, in community, and out into the world, through the power of the Spirit, to the worship and praise of God.

Having surveyed spirituality in our times, the current challenges facing us, and suggestions on how to move towards living spirituality, where do we go from here? A variety of forms, expressions, and approaches exist within the broad domain of Christian spirituality (historical, traditional, denominational, etc), and no doubt each has its place. However, instead of following any of these valuable directions, my primary focus will be on the canon of Scripture as our map for the journey ahead to our destination.

Part Two
Preparing For and Setting Out
on the Journey

3

The Map, Map Reading, and Living Spirituality

I have lived in the Swiss Alps for twenty-five years. Our chalet faces an impressive, seven-peaked mass of mountains—*les Dents du Midi*. In hiking up one of them, which I have done a number of times, it is crucial to have a map and to prepare in advance. I'm not talking about trailblazing here, but about following a prescribed, mapped-out route, recognizing signposts and landmarks, and aiming to arrive at my destination.

Having a map for our journey assists us in planning our path, potentially minimizing confusion, knowing our direction, and sometimes it may even contribute to saving a life. Yes, good preparation and a good map are helpful for arriving at our destination, although they are not a guarantee that all will go as planned.

It is important to realize that a journey might also include interesting detours or unpredictable dangers along the way. The path may be washed out. The fog may obscure the visibility. A thunderstorm may arise unexpectedly. We have to see how it develops as we go. A journey is like that.

Scripture and Theology

The need for Scripture as our map becomes clear as we reflect upon the two-fold challenge facing us: the rising attraction to cultural and non-Christian forms of spirituality on the one hand, and the impoverishment of Christian spirituality on the other. In order to respond to this two-fold challenge and to illuminate the path for the journey ahead, I am now ready to add another dimension to the basics of living spirituality that I developed in the previous chapter.

It is theological

Some of you may ask why I bother to include Scripture, a theological map, in the basic dimensions of spirituality. Can't we find our way to the destination without it? Doesn't spirituality run on its own and follow its own path? How can theological insights illuminate the path ahead?

As I understand it, theology is chiefly about the study of God and the Scripture. In turn, this study should profoundly impact how we progress in our journey toward God. If we are to find our way to living spirituality, diminish ambiguity, and contribute to reversing spiritual impoverishment, we need to be dependent on clear and incisive theological perspectives.

While it is true that theology is sometimes reduced to an object of scientific analysis or perceived as completely unrelated to spirituality, neither should be the case. Theology, as I see it, goes beyond science and has a deep and living connection to spirituality. That is to say, theology and spirituality ultimately refer to God, are connected to our personal knowledge of God, and are essential to our being in community with God and his people. We should see the final orientation and practical application of theology as a challenge to live spiritually, not merely to inform accurately.

As Christians, our spirituality requires a theological mapping for several reasons:

22

1. To come to sufficient understanding of God.

2. To find our spiritual bearings.

3. To holistically enlighten our hearts and minds.

4. To have a greater degree of objectivity in what we affirm
   and critique as truly or falsely spiritual.

5. To discern how to live the whole of life in community
   with God and each other in God's world.

Keep these reasons in mind as we go on. For now, let me add one
more important point. I believe the theological map is *related* to,
yet *distinct* from us. Let's consider why this essential configuration
is relevant to spirituality.

The map itself shows us that it lights our path, keeps our steps
steady and directs us in the way to life (Ps. 119:105). The map is
related to us in that it applies to our lives, but it is also distinct from
us in that it is God's revelation.

Far too often Christian spirituality is identified by the
assumption that the map means what it means "to us." This *may* be
the case, but equally it *may not*. How can we test our reading to see
if we're going in the right direction? We can easily end up
attempting to light our own path, and this creates problems.

Look at it this way. When the map is read only in relation to us
or with the impression that what *may* be the case *is* always the case,
we have the tendency to reduce our interpretation of the map to fit
our desires and wishes, instead of paying attention to what it
actually says and is. If there is no distinction or may not factor to be
alert to, we lose any potential for critique of our interpretation and
are left wide open for self-deception. We end up following what we
assume the path should be, although this assumption can in fact be
leading us in the wrong direction.

When we attempt to make it up as we go along, we face spiritual impoverishment, instead of enhancement. The *may not* possibility is important to consider, because wrong or inadequate interpretations of the map lead to diversions away from the path to life. These types of deviations are harmful and destructive to our spirituality. Let's face it, most of us aren't the best cartographers or trailblazers, and carving out our own path can frequently become extremely convoluted. We tend to go round in circles that lead us nowhere.

A better approach is to question, investigate, contemplate, and seek to follow the mapped out path in the clearest way possible. But this requires being attentive to *its* direction, *its* lighting, *its* perspectives and then how these apply to illuminating the path ahead for us.

The relation-distinction configuration when reading the map is crucial to have in place in order to diminish impoverishment and to further proceed on the journey of living spirituality. That is, the map stresses that it is revealed to us by God, and is not ours. To collapse these together, to solely turn the map into our own, will lead us astray and away from our destination.

As you seek to be living spirituality, it is vital to understand that neither you yourselves, nor the journey are the final authority: God and the map are. Think of it this way—your life and the way you live it are related to, but distinct from the map. Related in the sense that the map offers you information, direction, comfort, and insight; the way into community with God and community with each other and the world. Distinct in the sense that it is from God, and does not originate with you.

Imagine your life tethered to and directed by the scriptural map, which establishes the boundaries for and transcendent character of truth and spirituality. This configuration suggests that you are in a dialogical interaction that comprises you, the map, the Spirit, others, and the world. Yes, complexity again characterizes living spirituality. Dialogue is essential to counter those exclusive *make it*

24

up as you go along readings of the map and will contribute to reversing spiritual impoverishment. We must be cautious not to turn *Thy word is truth* into *our word is truth*.

A key focus of the journey is learning to read the map as accurately as possible so that its directives can be followed. It is crucial to develop skills that will help us be more objective in our approach so that in turn we can be more practical in our living.

These skills include a concern for the author and original audience, the literary, cultural, and historical context, as well as for the interpretation of the map for us. Map reading and living spirituality are not in separate compartments. They too are related and distinct. We desperately need to educate, equip, and inform people in our communities to practice the art of scriptural map reading in order to foster a deeper and ever increasing community with God.

In the previous chapters we've seen that there is often little or no concept of what *spirituality* means, particularly in Christian contexts. I believe we can begin to remedy this deficiency and reverse our impoverishment by carefully looking to the scriptural mapping, which offers the sufficient theological referent for our journey.

4

The Spirit is the Guide

We have seen so far that living spirituality is deeply connected to following Jesus and has four basic dimensions: holistic, interactive, interpretative, and theological. In setting out on the journey, it is also essential to have an accurate theological path illuminator. We have the map, but we also need a reliable and trustworthy guide who is familiar with the territory.

Without a Guide

High Alpine paths laced with wildflowers and green meadows are stunningly beautiful, but they can also be hazardous. Paths look alike, but lead in different directions. Although some paths may appear safe, they actually become risky or lead to dead ends. Or, paths may be partially covered in snow.

I well remember walking through a high mountain pass with my family one spring. Snow was still thawing, and we wondered if we were too high, too early. As we reached a critical point in the hike the path was covered in snow, and we weren't quite sure what was around the corner. Did the path carry on? As far as we could tell, the map indicated that it did. Was this just a wide section of snow located in one place, and after passing it the path would be clear again? We had to decide whether to go ahead or turn back.

The slope was quite steep and slipping on it could mean sliding straight down the mountainside. Being bold and somewhat careless, I forged ahead, determined to find out if the path continued around the corner, so as to not have to turn back. I began crossing the snow. There was no problem at first, but all of a sudden, the snow gave way. I shot straight down into a hole, literally disappearing from my family who had waited forty meters or so back.

I was fortunate. Instead of sliding down the slope, I was caught by a more solid, hard-packed snow. I only ended up with some cuts and bruises. After several rather tenuous moments, I struggled my way out of the hole and reappeared on the surface. That was the end of that. Needless to say, my relieved family and I turned back.

With a Guide

On such a path, a guide would have had more experience and wisdom as to the risks involved. A good guide will be attentive to levels of difficulty and to the goal of arriving safely at the final destination. I do not mean to imply by analogy that life will always go well because we have a guide, as this *may* or *may not* be the case.

While most of you reading this do not live in the Alps, you surely face numerous paths in life where perils abound. It is imperative to test the paths to the degree that we can, but we are also in need of a sure-footed guide. As we interpret the map for direction, it indicates that the Holy Spirit is the chief illuminator who will lead us on the right path ahead to our destination (1Cor. 12:1-3; Gal. 5:16-26).

We see this clearly in Romans 8:14, which so eloquently reminds us: those who are led by the Spirit are children of God. Paul has elaborated on the Spirit in this chapter, mentioning "Spirit" twenty-one times. The Spirit is no less than the Spirit of life, the

Spirit of testimony, and the Spirit of intercession. The apostle's primary focus, in this context, is not so much on *who* the Spirit is, but on what he *does* for those in Christ Jesus. Let's unpack this a bit further.

Paul first builds on the contrasts of verses 1-11 to fix the context for verse 14. He describes the Spirit of God as a life-giving Spirit in spite of death. Paul highlights the life-death contrast— because of the resurrection of the crucified One, living in the flesh leads to death, and living in the Spirit leads to life.

In verses 12-13 the apostle is concerned with the practical results of these contrasts he has just drawn out. Life in the Spirit is a daily, real-world life to be lived in a moment-by-moment trajectory. Paul does not write that Christians have no contact with sin, which he sees as the power sphere of the flesh. Rather, his point is that they are no longer ruled by the flesh, no longer belong to it, and no longer are to be imprisoned by it.

He goes on in verses 13-14 to confirm that those who will live are those who, by the Spirit, actively put to death the deeds of body as manifested by flesh. This is living by the Spirit and will result in life. The *"For"* explains it for us: for all who are led by the Spirit are children of God. The apostle is not talking about flashes of ecstatic encounters, but the steady guidance and mindset of the Spirit.

Misunderstanding the Holy Spirit

In our contemporary context however, with its diversity of maps and guides, there is a bewildering and powerful attraction to a *make it up as we go along* view of spirit. The broad availability of diverse spiritualities accompanied by the increasing levels of ambiguity and misunderstanding in our own circles, gives rise to a myriad of perplexing notions of *spirit*, which are connected to almost anything.

There are no limits or parameters to these kinds of logic. High ambiguity is what it's all about. Whatever s*pirit* is, it is utterly unbounded and undefined, and there is no way of identifying any of its substantial activities or core characteristics. The very thought of defining spirit is assumed to go against the nature of spirit; it is to remain vague and nebulous.

Think of expressions like, *the spirit of our times* or *the spirit of the film*. No one is quite sure what such a spirit is, but it is thought to have something to do with becoming aware of and recognizing the spirit in all things. For some this means that spirit is a concoction of new age and pagan forces focused on self-realization. Others emphasize that spirit—such as animal, river, mountain, and home spirits—make their presence felt as a sort of elusive and mystifying element that is interwoven into all things, appearing around every corner in mysterious ways. We may hear of spirit as ecstasy without argument or labyrinth without direction. Supposedly, the infinite, whatever that may be, is to be discovered everywhere. All that is finite has infinite spirit.

It is important to underscore that in such contemporary expressions of spirit we are left to our dreams and reveries, our personal opinions and feelings. So be it, many might say. Be creative. *Make it up as you go along.* Everyone has their own spirit and spirituality, and may define both in anyway they please.

Now let's look at another perspective. In theory, Christians acknowledge the importance of having the Bible as the map for the journey, but in practice they tend to ignore it in favor of the direct intervention and revelation of the Spirit. Personal immediacy and prompting are assumed to be more spiritual than carefully contemplating and following the map. And at what cost? In my view, the expense is spiritual impoverishment. There are an unfortunate set of similarities between some of the *make it up as we go along* views, and those operating in Christian circles. This should remind us of our tendency to falsely absolutize and of the need to be aware of the danger of self-deception.

Lamentably, biblical map studies often turn into mumbo jumbo, where similar degrees of ambiguity and an increasing reliance on the hyper-subjectivity that we find in non-Christian contexts, are prominent. Cultivated and honed map-reading skills that will help us to be living in the Spirit are on the wane, and regrettably have less and less to do with our views of spirituality.

Let's say you meet with twenty-four other people for a Bible study, and you all read the same part of the scriptural map. But then you all "discover" that the Spirit revealed a different interpretation of the map to each of you. And you all piously maintain that your perspective was given to you directly from the Spirit. That would mean that the Spirit is telling each of you to head off in different directions according to your own personal revelation. While this might be possible, it is highly unlikely. This view is closer to relativism than it is to the guidance of the Spirit. The high risk of interpretative self-deception here must not go unchecked.

All too often the focus in this context is ME. What the Spirit says to ME is central and important. This is partially true, but alas it is usually reduced to only ME and the Spirit, as the biblical map pales into growing insignificance. In this scenario, the Spirit does not help us navigate our way through the map and towards the best path: Jesus Christ and community with the living God. Rather, the Spirit tells ME individually and directly through what I experience what is in it for ME. The map, and Father, Son and Spirit play less and less of a role and it's ME and my path that counts. This well-meaning, but highly subjective and unmapped view of the Spirit, contributes to distressing levels of ambiguity and impoverished spirituality.

If this all sounds strange, that very strangeness shows us the dire state of our impoverishment. We are in danger of becoming so ME-focused, that we stray further and further from the map and the truly Spirit-illuminated path to life. It is essential to look to a new perspective.

A New Way

The map's perspective offers a markedly different portrayal. Explore John's gospel (especially chapters 13-16; or Romans 8, and 1 Corinthians 12-14, which are also key sections) and you will see the focus on the promise, work, witness, guidance, and gifting presence of the Holy Spirit.

Then take a more wide-angled survey. The New Testament shows us a number of significant directives that help reverse impoverishment and diminish ambiguity concerning the mapping of the Spirit. Let's briefly focus on a few central points.

The Holy Spirit is holy. This means he is holy in both character and divinity, as the Father and Son are holy and divine. This Spirit is unique as the Spirit of Father and Son, who is in intimate community with both. The Holy Spirit is revealed as the Spirit of truth who comes in Jesus' name so that his followers might have the blessing of being in community with Father, Son, Spirit, and each other. The dynamic community of God's life together makes living spirituality possible for us.

The Spirit is not some vague impersonal force or energy, or a guide without a map merely doing his own thing. In contrast, he is a personal agent whose actions are in harmony with the Father and Son, and who therefore is a capable guide in that he points us back to them, to the map, and how to live as we move toward our destination. Clearly, the Spirit and the map are to work together. The Spirit glorifies the risen Christ, acting as his very presence, illuminating the map in accordance with the directions that unfold for followers of Christ Jesus.

This mapped-out marker of the Spirit is a profound corrective to notions of spirit as an indefinable, directionless mass that is in all and for all. A spirit that flows through everything can only be referred to as *it*, and therefore loses the dimensions attributed to the Holy Spirit—personal community with Father, Son, ourselves, and others.

We are reminded again here of the reality of the relation and distinction configuration of the triune God. Father, Son, and Spirit are a divine, personal, and directed community—related, but also distinct. The Spirit in this configuration is a reliable and competent guide, who, as chief illuminator of the path to life, is capable of graciously and carefully leading us forward in our interpretation of the map. A *making it up as we go along* will lead us off course and into interpretative self-deception. Instead, careful study of the map is crucial to living in the Spirit, and reaching our destination.

Having shown you some of the benefits of Scripture as the map, and the Holy Spirit as our guide, I now want to take you through a selection of biblical texts and some community life stories that will highlight and develop living spirituality for our own journey. As I see it, credible theological insights and applicable stories will help direct us to our destination. In moving through this fascinating adventure, I am going to continue to remind you of the map and our location on it as we move through the journey. I will be attentive to the marked out path on the map, which is deeply connected with our own.

Part Three
Following the Map and the Guide

5

God, Creation, and Living Spirituality

My intention in the next chapters is to follow the map and the guide into a medley of markers that will lead us forward in the journey. A popular saying today, "It's about the journey, not the destination" is well known. In many contemporary contexts, the journey *is* the destination. People are satisfied with the mirage of an endless journey, but this is not what I have in mind. As I envision it, our journey is going somewhere, with God as its referent and a new heaven and earth as its final destination.

Finding our Bearings

Let's first find our bearings. To do this we want to focus on God, creation, and spirituality as *related to* and *distinct from* one another. This important theological configuration is crucial to living spirituality and will help us get situated. And why is it significant in this context? Because, as we have seen previously and now must stress again, one of the key features of the scriptural map and the community of Father, Son, and Spirit, is relation and distinction—a theological trajectory which has an impact on everything else leading to our destination.

Among other characteristics and attributes of God, relation and distinction are rooted in the community of Father, Son, and Spirit. Two points can be mentioned here. First, Father, Son, and Spirit are related to, but distinct from each other. This is one of the chief dynamics of their community together. They are all divine, yet not exactly so in all the same ways.

Second, because of this community, what we see in creation and human existence are marked by their traits and touched by their graces. That is, we see something of the relation and distinction of Father, Son, and Spirit revealed in many areas, including the magnificent complexity in nature and humans.

The significance of God as Creator, and as related to and distinct from creation, have not received the attention they deserve for configuring Christian spirituality. I intend to remedy that, and in the course of this chapter to contrast these two theological markers with contemporary and ancient expressions of spirituality. This theologically orientated, creational, relation-distinction perspective will open up possibilities for a new understanding of God, ourselves, spirituality, and the created world.

Now that we have our bearings, let's continue the journey.

God and Creation

To have a better perspective of living spirituality, I suggest that we begin in Genesis. If we consult the map of Scripture, we see that Genesis starts with God, Spirit, and creation.

Early Genesis affirms the word and action of the personal creator God creating what is there. Disclosure of the created world and an attestation that human beings are made as God's image come clearly into focus and provide a referent for the trajectory of the spiritual. God is portrayed as the creator of the whole masterpiece. And living spirituality, even at this early stage of the journey, is to be understood as depending on and benefiting from

God's majestic creation, as God reveals something of the spiritual in the material world he is creating.

Many expressions of spirituality today lead us in the wrong direction. In our contemporary context, "nature spiritualities" proliferate. We may even hear of the divinity or sanctity of nature and that everything is part of the divine. Another expression in evidence today proposes God has nothing to do with nature. This version of God and nature severs nature entirely from God, and leaves us to work it all out for ourselves. Both of these views fail to provide us with living spirituality. My concern will be primarily with the former, because it seems to breed greater ambiguity and therefore requires greater reversal. Let's understand why.

Nature spiritualities hold that nature is divine or is to be worshipped. I once heard the story of a fisherman who would say with each catch, "Oh, thank you great spirit of fish for giving this life to sustain mine." This type of statement is devoted to pantheistic notions and nature spirituality. That is, fish and humans are thought to be one and this oneness and unity is perceived to be ultimately interconnected with the divine spirit, which pervades all elements and facets of natural life. The divine is in everything and everything is in the divine.

I'm reminded here of another example. One morning a student and I were talking after my lecture on spirituality. Since we live in a small Alpine agricultural village, he chose the subject of farming, cows, and manure to make his point. He told me, "When I dig manure I'm one with it as I'm one with God, the cows, grass, and everything."

I responded, "It seems unlikely that I could be standing here having a discussion with manure. The last time I dug manure, it didn't talk back to me."

This fellow wanted to see everything as related, linked up, and interconnected. He left no room for distinction. The truth is, as much as he may be *related* to manure in that he is digging it, he is also quite clearly *distinct* from it in that he *is not* the manure.

In his view, the divine and nature are understood to be one and the same: the suppleness and flexibility of the divine stretches beyond demarcation. There are no boundaries or modes of distinction anywhere. Nature, however, from the Genesis mapping's point of view, is not divine. It is created. The fish, in the example above, do not by the great spirit give themselves to our bait; they are simply caught by it. Nor is it possible to have relation without distinction by assuming to be *one* in seamless conformity with the impersonal, as in the case of the manure.

Notice in the Genesis 1 and 2 mapping (now would be a good time to open your Bible and study these chapters) there is no confusion, in contrast to many versions of spirituality today, between the Creator and the created. In Genesis, God is not nature, nor is God confused with it. Genesis depicts God as involved with nature, but God is never portrayed as entirely related to or distinct from the created world.

This is an important clarification for at least two reasons. First, and more generally, it begins to diminish spirituality confusion. It reveals something of who God is, something of who we are, and something of what nature is: God is Creator and not nature, humans are not God or nature, and nature is created not Creator. Second, and more specifically, the clarification allows us to contest theologies and spiritualities that speak of God as being entirely one with the created world (related) or having utterly nothing to do with it at all (distinct). How then are we to view the created? And how do we view God, the royal architect of this creation?

In the early part of the Genesis narrative, we read that the personal God who is there is the Creator of the world. Creation exists because this particular God created it. It has a sanctity, but not of its own. Creation, therefore, is special and central for many reasons, most notably because it is created with purpose and a godly personal touch.

There is a clear biblical mandate for respecting creation, caring for it based on God's actions, and enabling creation to fulfill its aims of praising God. But the created is not God. The soil, sun and moon, animals and humans are distinct from God, and they are not divine. And God as the divine is not some impersonal force or energy aligned with everything else, but a set-apart, personal God, who creates, makes covenants, and speaks and acts within creation in an ongoing way. We should not think of God as caught up in the created world or exclusively identified by it. God is the great actor and responder who exists in distinction from all that is created.

At the emergence of creation, God is the divine transcendent One who imminently orchestrates a symphony of words. These words become vehicles of creating something aesthetically marvelous and intricately complex, though not free of risk. Creation is a wild and diverse marvel, a purposefully directed wonder of wonders, and God is the speaking sculptor who says and it becomes. This God, the Genesis God, is the God who sees, replies to, and proclaims that what is created is *good*.

Again, God is related to creation and God is distinct from creation. When Christians ignore one or the other of these two truths they do so at their own theological and spiritual peril. This dual-truth perspective is both helpful in the sense that it opens up possibilities for a more holistic, interactive, interpretative, and theologically-based (our basic dimensions) spirituality through this significant configuration between God and creation. It is also thought provoking because it becomes more difficult to put God or creation into a box of our own making. These two simultaneous truths begin to reverse spiritual impoverishment and to illuminate the path ahead. To focus on an "either/or" perspective, in this context, heightens the danger of misunderstanding God, the scriptural map, creation, ourselves, and ultimately our spirituality.

God, the Created World, and Humans

Another significant directive on the theological map I wish to highlight, is that God is not entirely comparable to the many other ancient Near Eastern accounts of gods that pre-date or are contemporary with Genesis. The theologies of these other maps have the gods creating the world through magical incantations and divine battles. Consider *The Creation Epic* (Tablet IV & V - date undecided, but likely second millennium BC):

> Against Anshar, king of the gods, though seekest evil
> (against) the gods,
> my fathers thou hast confirmed wickedness
> (though) drawn up thy forces, girded on thy weapons.
> Stand thou up, that I and thou meet in single combat.
> When Tiamat heard this,
> She was like one possessed; she took leave of her senses.
> In fury Tiamat cried aloud.
> To the roots her legs shook both together.
> She recites a charm, keeps casting her spell,
> while the gods of battle sharpen their weapons.
> Then joined issue Tiamat and Marduk, wisest of gods.
> They strove in single combat, locked in battle. (Tablet IV)
>
> When he had vanquished and subdued his adversaries
>
> He constructed stations for the gods
> He determined the year by designating the zones.
> After he had appointed the days
> the precincts of night and day
> Taking the spittle of Tiamat Marduk created.
> He formed the clouds and filled them with water.
>
> Thus he covered the heavens and established the earth
> So he created heaven and earth. (Tablet V)

Although the narrative mapping in Genesis uses some of the language and comparable imagery of other creation accounts, the differences outweigh the similarities. The uniqueness of this God and his creation are prominent on the scriptural map, affirming a radical distinction from all polytheistic descriptions. The God of the Genesis narrative is not a divine magician, nor in competition with other divinities. Rather, he is a provocative personal Creator who is not one among many.

In contrast to other ancient Near Eastern creation stories, the beginning of Genesis involves no magic and no battles between the gods for power and influence. Early Genesis concentrates on God, creation, the creative word-act-response, and the presence of the Spirit. God and Spirit together, and in relational accord, bring about that which was not. And they bring it about as *good*.

There is another striking feature of creation: God is the Creator of human beings. Striking? Yes, because these beings, a man and a woman—Adam and Eve—are said to be created as God's images. They are special and skillfully crafted. They possess unique awareness, and there is nothing else in all creation quite like them. Though they are a pair of images, each is individually hewn and creatively assembled for community with God, one another, and the created world.

Some accounts of human creation portray the gods creating humans to do their work, as is the case with *The Creation Epic:*

> When Marduk hears the words of the gods
> his heart prompts (him) to fashion artful works
> opening his mouth he addresses Ea
> to impart the plan he had conceived in his heart:
> "Blood I will mass and cause bones to be.
> I will establish a savage, 'man' shall be his name.
> Verily, savage-man I will create.
> He shall be charged with the service of the gods
> that they might be at ease." (Tablet IV)

41

But the Genesis narrative affirms that God has created a *good* creation *for* these being-images. What a remarkable difference. Humans become the only creatures in all creation who have the capacity to be in intimate community with God. They also have the freedom to accept or reject what God graciously offers to them.

In this light, we are to view humans creationally as spiritual beings: they image God; they are infused with the breath-spirit of God. This creation spirituality is expressed through human, flesh-and-blood existence and opens possibilities in the domains of community, relationship, love, work, sacrifice, creativity and responsibility to be lived out into a created world. We find nothing like the remarkable Genesis creation story anywhere else.

The Genesis God is the artist of life, the personal *good* Creator, who is related to and distinct from the created. This God created humans in his image, providing them with a *good* creation. Early Genesis mapping sets out, among other things, to critique the prominent ancient Near Eastern views of the deity of nature and the deity of human beings. Neither is divine, but both are created.

Many ancient and contemporary versions of spirituality and creation require lofty degrees of subjectivity to sustain them. They fall far short of having the capacity to theologically inform and transform our views of a world that is not our own. That is, the emphasis on subjectivity is too great, and in being so it pays insufficient attention to the objective character of God and a Genesis mapping of the created world, which has the capacity to override and explain our subjectivity.

Let's put it this way: God's world forces itself upon us. It puts us in our place. We are a marvel, but we are broken and far from being God. As such, Christians should confess dependence on God and creation, as both are capable of integrating—but also surpassing—our subjectivity, thereby giving it true meaning and significance.

Now I hope you see that the God of Scripture is unique when compared to nature spirituality or the other ancient Near Eastern perspectives of gods, the creation of the world, and human beings. Theologically, creationally, and spiritually, the biblical God alone is God the Creator. I also hope you noticed that humans are special. They are creatures unlike any others. Referred to as God's images, humans are remarkably capable of a deep level of community with God, each other, and creation.

Keeping these essentials in mind, let us move on to understand the value of a creational perspective with respect to two problems that frequently occur when Christians discount the importance of creation for spirituality.

6

Problems of Disregarding Creator and Creation: Towards a New Perspective

When we disregard either the *good* Creator or creation and their illumination of the path to living spirituality, significant degrees of spiritual impoverishment will be experienced. In this chapter, a new perspective will be developed to reverse this, and to move us in a better direction.

Problem 1: The Banalization of Good

This first problem has to do with the tendency to banalize good in the face of evil. That is, to be so devastated by problems concerning evil that there is little or no attention given to good. In my work here at L'Abri, I have repeatedly seen this problem expressed in the lives of many people, and struggle with it myself.

Let's face it, there is an apparent poverty of goodness in the world. As we encounter the overwhelming darkness of evil in our lives, the light of God's goodness may seem all too frequently to disappear. But does it? I think that Christians may often overlook the double affirmation early in the Genesis narrative: God and creation are *good*. I well remember this lack in one student's life.

Kevin's Story

Kevin had grown up in a Christian family, believed in God and committed his life to Christ. He had Christian friends, belonged to a youth group, and had done well in school. In the view of many in his church, Kevin's life was stable, upright, and exemplary.

When he went away to college, he was challenged with new views and experiences. Kevin found himself faced with questions that he had never before considered. Other students and professors pressured him: if God is good, why is there so much evil? Where does evil come from? Maybe God, if there is a God, is silent. And if God were silent, then humanity would become the creator and ultimately decide if something was good or evil.

Kevin had never thought about why he believed God was good. He realized that he had merely taken it for granted. In the midst of questions and struggles, he sensed he was carrying the world's evil on his shoulders. It didn't help that around this time a close and trustworthy friend died, while another maliciously betrayed him.

These circumstances led him to despair, frustration, and a sense of abandonment. He found that he had very few resources to support his views of God's goodness. His community with God and God's people drastically decreased.

Unfortunate but not uncommon, Kevin's response was to reject much of his past and his beliefs about God. While this may be entirely appropriate in some cases, Kevin was ill-equipped to critically sift through his faith. That meant he was unable to identify certain past beliefs that were true and important to keep, while also unable to criticize other beliefs that might need to be replaced. The goodness of God belongs to the former—a true belief worth holding close.

Serious doubts about God and God's goodness began to eat away at Kevin's faith. Doubt is not always negative unless it turns into unbelief and Kevin was not quite there yet. But his grades began to fall, and he began to drink excessively and to take various drugs. He asked God to help him get his life back on track, but grew weary and felt as if prayer were pointless. His intense struggle with the problem of evil and the goodness of God was undoing him.

When Kevin came to the L'Abri community he was thoroughly perplexed and honest enough to admit it. I believe that God was working in his life and have no doubt that was part of the reason he was here with us in Switzerland. Kevin was seeking answers, particularly to this most complex question about good and evil and generally to a host of other questions. As I tutored him, he gradually opened up through times of lengthy discussion, helpful study material, and life in the community.

We talked about many things, but eventually his pressing concern emerged: is there any good at all? And if there is, how might we agree on what it is? In other words, Kevin was facing what I will call the *problem of good*. To focus on the problem of evil is to already embrace some standard of good, but where does such a notion of good come from and how is it to be defined? I believe that Kevin, like many of us, had a tendency to banalize good in the face of the power of evil.

Creational goodness

As evil as evil may be, the scriptural map shows that God claims to be the creative source and origin of good. One way of envisioning this is the affirmation that there is no way of saying anything is good without good having some independent status apart from us. And that status is ultimately found in God. The reality of good is an actuality that we assume, trust, and embrace as we go about our daily lives, although no one escapes the horror, power and impact of evil.

Furthermore God, as creational, personal good precedes personal evil, thereby restricting it to a parasitic status. Though personal and parasitic, evil must borrow from that which is not its own, and therefore it is not original. If evil was not able to be compared to anything good, it wouldn't be evil. And it is because we have a way of comparing that we can identify something as evil.

In addition to these claims concerning God and goodness, God has already done, is doing, and will redemptively do something to bring about the end of evil. We find expression of this most clearly in the biblical covenants, the coming of the Kingdom of God, the life, death, and resurrection of Christ, the outpouring of the Spirit, and the future day of final reckoning.

These truths of God's creational goodness, a salvific trajectory, spirit empowerment, and the promise of the ultimate defeat of evil do not explain everything. But they do give us a sufficient foundation upon which to build a stronger and better belief in God's goodness.

This is not to say that the struggle with good and evil disappears from the Christian life. Evil remains baffling, hideous, and sometimes inconceivable, while good calls us from the depths of despair reinforcing its virtuosity in mysterious and powerful ways. As Christians we must move forward in trust and hope that are grounded in the revelation and character of God, which points to the origin and finality of good.

In a world of proliferating brokenness, radical evil, and convoluted spirituality, we now face a desperate urgency to stress the biblical claims of the primacy of a good and personal Creator God— the God who is there. It is important to notice that this is where we momentarily set aside the notion of *relation* and *distinction*—the "both/and" perspective—and are presented with an "either/or" perspective. Let me clarify.

Good and evil: Either/or

To look at God and creation with the map in hand is to see them as *either* good *or* not good. This either/or argues that God and the Genesis creation cannot be good *and* evil. Any such configuration fails to represent a biblical point of view and lacks a sufficient correspondence to life as we know it. In the human context, for example, good and evil are simply not entirely mixed. End of story. Most of us live by and make value judgments, which therefore presuppose some credible distinction between the two.

In considering God's goodness, I want to point out that this attribute is affirmed at the beginning of the creation story and develops from there. Scripture clearly celebrates God's goodness and the goodness of creation, and in turn this should also be a priority for Christians.

When we endorse and enact these truths, we will still find a place for proclaiming the origin of goodness over evil, a creational affirmation over negation, trust over suspicion, and life over death. From the scriptural map and its creational perspective, evil, negation, suspicion, and death are always second-order discourse and can never ultimately be the context for themselves. That is, goodness, trust, and life are always already there in the first place.

When we consider non-Christian expressions of spirituality, including the kitsch of religious trinkets, or the postmodern *khora*, it is crucial to remember that first order discourse states: no one ever goes beyond, behind, or entirely surpasses the depths of goodness. The inexhaustibility and origin of goodness are located in God and therefore transcend all limits.

Kevin grew convinced that this made considerably more sense than accusing God of not being good on God's own standards of goodness. And that goodness was part of his life and the world in which he lived. Such an acknowledgement was one of his first steps on the way toward living spirituality.

Combating evil

As Christians we have often become so dangerously conditioned to evil and to a world that believes God is silent, that we may fail to recognize that the origin and irruptions of goodness are more profound than the deepest evil. Prior to all else, living spirituality is grounded in community with this particular Creator God who is good and who has created a good creation.

These truths and realities should lead us to carefully consider that while it is worthwhile and sometimes even essential to grapple with the weighty problems of good and evil, there comes a time when it is necessary to move from the speculation mode of "why", to the response mode of combating evil. God's being and dedication to good, and our devotion to God and living spirituality call for nothing less.

This is not to say that the questions concerning good and evil disappear or become irrelevant. Not at all. These questions remain perplexing, although the time and energy spent on resolving them should decrease, as *action* against evil increases. Such action can and should have a variety of expressions including prayer, thanksgiving, and worship, comforting the oppressed, feeding the poor, sheltering the weak, giving voice to the victim, and restraining the exploits of the abuser, among a host of other commitments.

Problem 2: Salvation Alone?

A second and different sort of problem that arises when we neglect a good creation and a good God is that we too often embrace an exclusively salvific outlook in exchange for a creational one. There is no emphasis on God as Creator or creation. What does such a Creator-creation oversight look like, and why does it produce impoverished spirituality in contrast to living spirituality?

Linda's story
Linda was a young woman in her twenties who came to L'Abri to deepen her faith. She had been a Christian for a couple of years, was a popular person, a good student, a reader of the Bible, and interested in spirituality.

Linda had been taught a restrictively salvific perspective of Christianity in her church. Of course, this is not entirely a bad thing. But as a result of this teaching, Linda was left with an incomplete biblical perspective from which to live spirituality. Let me explain.

Living spirituality is concerned with the whole of life and an adequate holistic, interactive, interpretative, theologically based spirituality, not merely salvation in Christ. Linda had forgotten to read the map more broadly and to integrate Genesis with the rest of Scripture and her life. For her, the creator God and creation had no positive connection to salvation, and therefore had little place in her view of spirituality.

Linda failed to see the relevance of a good creation and its impact in all areas of life. She had decided that there was little need for Christian engagement with the material world. This spiritual limitation produced taboos and instilled fears in her that were far from living spirituality. Linda dared not listen to anything but Christian music, felt she should have only Christian friends, and that she could do only Christian work. She was taught that only the saved had any worth whatsoever. Such a narrow view became ingrained in her and severed her from so much of life that is important, relevant, and worth participating in.

In spite of evil and sin, creation was and is primarily good. Scripture and living spirituality affirm that there are diverse areas of life that merit Christian involvement and that all human beings have worth and the capacity to do some good. Many people do what Scripture describes as good things: feed the poor, help the sick, comfort the oppressed and so on. But this good is never good enough for people to declare themselves righteous before God.

Passages in Scripture like Romans 3 chiefly target those who believe that they are good enough to have a claim on God through race, creed, law, church denomination, or right action. These people try to put God in their debt. They proudly proclaim, "God look at me, I'm good and have done good. You are obliged to declare me righteous. God you owe me."

No one, absolutely no one, has the right to say this. Yet humans are not devoid of good or incapable of doing good. Creation attributes significance, worth, affirmation, and some capacity to do good to all humans, while also providing a robust theology for living spirituality that relates to the whole of life, not merely the salvific.

In Linda's case, where salvation had taken a hyper-dominant position, creation was disregarded and relegated to insignificance. Clearly, there is no question that salvation in Jesus Christ has a central place on the map, yet it is not be confused with or to take the place of creation. Let's consider this.

Salvation in context

If there is no distinction between salvation and the rest of God's works and ways, then theology and spirituality get truncated. Christians, at this stage, are in danger of losing the important feature of a theological relation and distinction grounded in the character of God.

The saving work of Christ finds its rightful place as a dynamic site on the map. Yet there is a dilemma: salvation alone is an inadequate explanation for the origin and destination of Christian spirituality.

That is, the scripturally ordered and historical unfolding of salvation reveals to us that salvation comes into a context: God's existence, a created world, death, covenant, a people, a culture, a time—all of which precede the incarnated person and mission of Jesus. God's salvific act dramatically portrayed in and through the sending of Christ finds its first and wider context in the primacy of God's act of creation: a created world affirmed by God and including humans in community with their Creator.

Through the power of the Spirit in connection with the map, intense dialogue and personal study, Linda eventually revised her views. She came to realize that a creational perspective offers a truer and more wide-ranging theology and spirituality. To live spirituality is to be reminded that God the personal Creator is there, the world is God's good creation, and that human beings have creational worth and value as images of God. Living spirituality is deeply rooted in the truth that, "In the beginning God created . . . ."

This revision led Linda to a stronger faith and enabled her to see Christian spirituality as engaging a variety of concerns, including politics, art, economics, social work, mission, and business. Her world exploded. A creational-salvific spirituality is to be strongly connected to the whole of life. Linda began to embrace living spirituality as an adventure of community with the living God, his people, and the world. And this opened up the path to life.

In order to counter the problems of disregarding a creational spirituality, we who follow Christ will want to live in the light of a new perspective, which comprises creational truths. These mapped-out truths set the context for understanding the rest of theology and spirituality. When we do live them out, impoverished views of Christian spirituality begin to diminish, and the path ahead is illuminated.

Let's review where we are in respect to God, creation, and the two problems we've explored. Remember, Genesis claims that the personal God who is there has created a good and extraordinary world for human beings who are God's images.

This direction-orientated and precision-crafted creation, sculpted in time with human images, is the act of the mighty Creator. God is not nature and creation is not spirituality, but each is related to and distinct from each other.

We have seen the considerable lack of adequate theological referents in the market place of some ancient and contemporary forms of spirituality. The referent for spirituality is tremendously important. High levels of ambiguity and inadequate referents can and do produce impoverished forms of spirituality. God and God's creation deserve, even demand, their rightful place as we seek to theologically configure a Christian spirituality and to practically live it individually, in community, and out into the world.

An authentic human and personal experience of community with God, through the living Christ and in the power of the Spirit is essential, but a referent for Christian experience, above and beyond that experience, is primary.

In light of this, Christians are to maintain a critical distance from counterfeit referents such as new age thought, idolatry, and astrology, or other sorts of cryptic and dying spiritualities, which are all too readily touted today as ways of a true spiritual life.

The crucial theological question is central. Our concern here is not with something that we feel or experience as "beyond" or "transcendent," but with the issue of *who* is speaking and acting, *who* is calling, and *who* is addressing us. Of course, impersonal entities neither speak nor act, and if we have little or no accurate information about the referent of our spirituality, we should have some serious questions. A real and genuine spiritual connection, through the redemptive work of the crucified One, to the personal God who is actually there beyond me, results in release from sin, a changed heart, and a transformed mind—life amidst the divine community.

We have also seen that the theological dimension of God's character and creation affirm an understanding that God is good and that the field of living spirituality is the whole of life. Our spirituality, as a result, is to be lived as a holistic, interactive, interpretative and theological adventure set within and enhanced by creation.

A Christian view of spirituality affirms the truth that there is a creational spirituality. The created world is a world that we are to explore, care for, and sustain. Living and true spirituality does not reject the material world, but engages it in service of God. Christians are to participate in the world and contribute to bringing goodness to all areas of life. As God has not left creation or humans to desolation, decay, or ultimate death, neither should we consent to dying forms of spirituality that have no capacity to redeem the created.

I cannot stress enough the magnitude of viewing relation and distinction as rooted in the character and person of the infinite God. God, creation, and spirituality are related, while also being distinct. If we are to diminish spiritual impoverishment and high levels of ambiguity, these three should not be collapsed into each other. A theological notion of relation and distinction in dialogue is vital to a Christian worldview and living spirituality. Rather than leading us further from God's truth, such a configuration brings us closer to it.

7

Living Spirituality in Brokenness:
The Path to Redemption

The post-creation biblical mapping in Genesis tells us of the dramatic results of broken community with God. As the journey continues in this chapter, the two images of God—Adam and Eve— do not resist the temptation of the talking serpent. Life with God, and all that it comprises, is devastatingly altered. Yet God, the master cartographer, will illuminate the path to redemption.

Notice (now would be a good time to open your Bible and study this chapter) that the serpent is created as part of what the Lord God had made (Gen 3:1). God and the serpent are not equals, and the Genesis narrator wants readers to know that. The talking serpent is cunning, but it is a creature and not to be equated with the Creator.

A dialogue then begins between Eve and the serpent, who is both truth-teller (the images *will* indeed be like God knowing good and evil) and liar (the images *will* die 3:4-5, 3:22). Unlike God who is exclusively truth-teller, the serpent with a double identity deceptively attempts to usurp and counterfeit God's original artistry. God, the artist of life, is questioned and undermined, and the talking serpent—as the fraudulent engineer of such a maneuver in this creational context—instigates death with God.

Death with God? The Adam and Eve images, who fall for the false representations of the serpent, are consequently deprived of the garden and from having any access to the tree of life (3:21-24). The splendor of what was formerly an exceptional community is compromised and at risk. Death with God will produce awful consequences, although God continues to provide (3:21) in spite of this radical change. As rebellion against God proliferates, sin will turn the human cultivation of the earth into its pollution—into a disfiguring of creation's capacity to praise God.

The talking serpent with the double identity has attempted to produce a re-framing of creation. Twisting in and around it, the serpent seeks to apply excessive pressure, endangering creation's majesty and ultimately its very survival. And survival, unfortunately, becomes a major part of what creation and life are all about.

The Marks of Redemption

Let's shift our view from God and creation to focus more intently on spirituality as it now develops in the face of death with God. As we do so, remember that in a Christian perspective, creation and spirituality are related and distinct: complementary, but not the same.

In order to continue to follow the map after creation and to further illumine the path for the journey, I am now ready to add another dimension to the basics of living spirituality that were developed in previous chapters.

It is redemptive
The drama of redemption begins to unfold and lead us forward. We will be looking at several redemption markers on the map in order to explore how the path leads us to our destination: the trajectory of

covenant toward kingdom in this chapter and the arrival of the Messiah and the Kingdom of God in the next. As we examine these two interrelated parts of the map, the path will illumine further.

The Covenant moves Toward the Kingdom of God

In the unfolding post-creation in Genesis, we see the proliferation of evil, followed by de-creation, and subsequently by re-creation. God grieved and filled with heartache (Gen. 6:6), will flood the earth. But just before doing so, God finds favor with Noah, a righteous one. All will not be lost in the ensuing drama, and creation will continue. This choice leads God to establish a covenant (Gen. 6:18) and to save Noah's family from the impending catastrophic consequences in an attempt to re-establish community. God will be involved in both redrawing creation and further developing living spirituality as covenant community, on behalf of humanity and creation. Post-flood, Genesis repeats something of the promise of covenant blessing and creation ordinances (Gen. 9) that had been given to the first two human images: Adam and Eve (Gen. 1-2).

After the flood, God continues to reveal his rule in covenant-making, blessing, and eradicating sin. We begin to discover that God is a promise-making God. Later, God makes a covenant with Abram to bless and be a blessing to all the peoples of the earth (Gen. 12-22). Abraham and Sarah's offspring are to be as numerous as the stars in the sky. It is through God's promise to them that the child Isaac is born and subsequently the nation of Israel founded and substantiated. God's plan to have a people through whom the revelation and representation of God would come starts to take shape.

Israel was to be God's nation. God, therefore, was not only the Creator of creation, but became King of the state of Israel. God, the King, would use this nation not only to reveal something of his character and purpose, but also to continually establish a redemptive yet warrior-like rule over anti-God powers and agents in order to bring forth his ultimate kingdom.

Through the great act of liberation at the Exodus, the people of Israel will enter into another covenant with their King (Ex. 20-23). God has heard their cry and acts to establish a just rule on both his and their behalf. The people are redeemed from slavery in Egypt, given the law, and are eventually to be brought into the promised land.

Exodus remains a central and remarkable phase in the self-revelation of God and the life of God's people and living spirituality is never far from this founding event. *Live and remember the Exodus*, because God has intervened in a radical manner to redeem and liberate his people. "I am the Lord your God, who brought you out of the land of Egypt." (Ex. 20:2).

In this post-exodus redemption setting, God arranges the bi-lateral covenant of the law and dwells in the midst of the people. God also graciously institutes a sacrificial system with the capacity to make temporal atonement for lawbreaking possible. This allows Israel, in the midst of sin, to engage in ongoing community with the Almighty, who is portrayed as the Holy One, the great *I am*.

Israel the nation, ruled by God, judges and priests, then demands a human king. Eventually they move from tribal state, to kingship, to divided monarchy, and to then to exile into the hands of the Babylonians. Throughout this there is a cycle of covenant making and breaking from which emerges the treasure store of Wisdom literature and the Psalms—precious resources for the vocation of living spirituality. Let's explore this further.

Wisdom emerges. It invites reflection, question, and struggle. It covers everything from advice on how to take care of daily tasks, to the absurdity of them all. Wisdom, without the illumination of the fear of the Lord, loses its way. For true wisdom relates to living spirituality as it deals with facing life in all its ups and downs.

Here's how it goes. God graciously meets us through living as we shape the contours of daily routines and choices, so that we might learn to wisely follow the path to life. The fear (awe, reverence) of the Lord is the beginning of wisdom. This saying targets a two-dimensional reality: wisdom as internal, focused on the individual, and as external, situated in a variety of social contexts in the world. Life is to be filled with the gift of the wisdom of God, which applies to the whole of human activity as we forge ahead on the journey.

The poetry of the Psalms, in turn, addresses us as a bundle of life in community with God. While God, Psalmist and Israel wrestle, darkness hovers over the landscape of life. Light escapes, but is captured again when God graciously illumines the path ahead. In the covenantal mapping literature of the Psalms, we find powerful claims of trust and gratitude mixed with disclosures of deep despair and estrangement.

In the Psalms we see creational affirmations and covenant shattering, combined with a longing for a renewal of relational safety and stability. As the Psalmist might cry out, *May your goodness, oh God, shine through and lament not be our lot in life. Lord keep us by your side in the land of the living.*

Living spiritually is enhanced and enriched through the Psalms and their frequent affirmations of and appeals to God's covenant loyalty. Many of these writings, however, may shock us with their realism. In the midst of our sometimes *automatic pilot* spirituality, where everything is supposedly bright and happy, some of the Psalms remind us that community with God and the path to life are far from straight forward.

There is and will be brokenness, mystery, dark times, judgment, desperate searching, and much more. Though these circumstances frequently lead to illumination and new understanding, arriving there means going through—not taking a detour around—facets of spirituality that may not fit our desired schemes, notions, and expectations of God. The path may become difficult and the destination may seem far away, but God is faithful to lead us forward. The Psalms are a richly textured slice of life with God, and they offer us revelatory insights into humanness and living spirituality.

Later on in the journey, post-Psalms, God speaks powerfully through the prophets. The people of God are breaking covenant and disfiguring community with their God. They have forgotten the Exodus and are now characterized by their ignorance, betrayal, affluence, idolatry, dishonesty, and the banalizing of truth. Unless they reform, they are headed for the valley of slaughter, death, and desolation (Jer. 7: 30-34).

The Prophets proclaim God's judgment and call for a new vision of spiritual reality. They intensely mourn the loss of community with God and offer a severe critique of the life of God's people. They attempt to shake these people from their complacency and radical sinfulness in order to make them aware of their covenant responsibilities so that they might return to God and live.

Prophetic pronouncements, however, not only affirm judgment and the impending exile for covenant breaking, but also the grace and mercy of God in the eventual restoration of Israel and a new covenant—a new Israel made up of every tongue and tribe. This happens as the superabundance of God's grace—couched in vivid creational terms—overflows in forgiveness and restoration (Jer. 31:31-40). And then we begin to see the perceptible silhouette of a Messiah figure who will come more fully into view to establish God's Kingdom through love, justice, release from sin, and salvation (Isa. 52:1-53:12).

Let's review how far we've come. Covenant remains a significant signpost for spirituality today. We should not ignore this illumination of the path for the journey as we trace the trajectory of the people of God who have come before us. Spirituality along with community with God for the people of Israel—and for Christians in general—has deep roots in creation and God's specific covenant promises.

Covenant is a way of creating community, stability, and alliance. It is the way of God. Yet the Psalms and Prophets have shown us how God's people miserably fail to align themselves with God's covenant purposes and are subsequently judged. At the same time, we have seen that God is a God of promise who is gracious and loving, keeping the covenant to bless and redeem his people.

As God is revealed through covenant as merciful and just, his people are to reflect this in the way they live individually, in community, and in the world. Christians are to be holy, unique, and set apart as we represent God. To be spiritual, in this sense, is to be living in covenant community with God and his people, and to have this reality affect the whole of our lives. Quite practically, this means that our daily living originates from and returns to this community as the central referent for everything else that we say and do.

Covenant illumines the path by telling us something about God and his willingness to be faithful, reveal, promise, judge, and act graciously in love to form a people for himself. But covenant also specifically informs us about how to live and to walk in the ways of God in the land of the living. Walking in the ways of God includes being thankful, just, ever-vigilant concerning the perils of dying spiritualities, and loving God and our neighbor.

There is no simple formula here that will give us life and truth. What we *do* is deeply rooted in who we *are*: beloved children of God and sinners. In the midst of sin and failure (covenant breaking) on the journey, God remains faithful to his promises to inaugurate a new covenant so that community with him might be offered to all.

We have moved through some of the theological and interpersonal dynamics of covenant which help us move forward on the journey. At this point, however, the map becomes somewhat unclear. Has the journey come to an end? Where does the path go from here?

Israel longs for God to illumine the path again, but the sting of the ongoing reality of exile burns with deferral. Israel laments: *Why, O God, is the kingdom not arriving? Where are You? When will You come to restore and reinstate your people?*

8

The Messiah and the Kingdom of God: Redemption Arrives

After a long period of time, rife with measures to discern God's renewed activity, John the Baptist arrives creating an intense commotion. He boldly announces the Kingdom of God is near, signaling that God is again illuminating the path ahead for the journey.

With the proclamation of the Kingdom of God, the old covenant transfers to the prophesied new: redemption arrives. Looking once again at the map (now would be a good time to open your Bible and to study these chapters) we see in the gospel of Matthew (3-4) that the Baptist is the one about whom the great prophet Isaiah speaks. Matthew says that John will precede the vital manifestation of God's rule in the arrival of the Messiah, who will come to establish this rule in mercy, justice, and salvation.

In the incarnation of Jesus there is a powerful declaration of war against evil—God's *end-time* rule is disclosed. Incarnation further sets the stage for the battle between God and Satan, while also having a profound redemptive impact on tarnished creation.

Jesus, however, is not merely born. He is baptized, receives the Spirit, resists Satan, proclaims the fulfillment of the old covenant, and inaugurates the new. He brings an end to Israel's exile, performs creational/nature miracles, and proclaims the Kingdom of God has arrived. He *is* and *does* the good news as only God could.

If we read Matthew 3-4 carefully, we see that John the Baptist, as many Jews of his time, was expecting a Messiah who would both vindicate the righteous and punish the evil. Notice that John proclaims that he baptizes with water, but one more powerful than he is coming who will baptize in the Holy Spirit and fire. This is the Messiah. He is the one who has a winnowing fork in his hand. He will clear the threshing floor, gathering the wheat into the barn and burning up the chaff with fire (3:11-12). John, as the long-awaited spokesperson of God, announces blessing and judgment and prepares the way of the Lord.

The life, mission, and teaching of Jesus become the ultimate map marker on the journey. As it is mapped out in the gospel of Matthew, immediately after his baptism and Spirit reception, Jesus is tempted by the devil and deftly refutes his evil offers. In so doing, he defies Satan, begins to invade his territory and stronghold, thus signifying that God's rule is breaking in to defeat death and to bring about redemption.

As his public ministry begins, Jesus proclaims John's, "Repent for the Kingdom of heaven [God] is at hand" (4:17). This is followed by a long series of teaching in the Sermon on the Mount (5:1-7:29) that more clearly identifies that the Kingdom of God has arrived, that Jesus is the Messiah, and that there is a new offer to be in community with him. To be living spirituality is to be living in and under the Kingdom of God as the explosive character of the Sermon reveals. The authority and teaching of Jesus is striking, and hearing and acting upon it leads us to the path of life.

But later in the gospel of Matthew we read that John the Baptist is not entirely convinced. As he sits in prison he no doubt wonders where the further manifestation of blessing/judgment is.

The response to such concern and perplexity is found in Matthew 11:

Yes, Jesus says, I am the one. Tell John that the deaf hear, the blind see, the lame walk, the lepers are healed, the dead are raised and the good news is preached to the poor. *Contemplate this truth attentively.*

Why did Jesus come? The previous confirmation to John is set in the context of the Old Testament and the eventual arrival of the Messiah who would bring the Kingdom of God and a fulfillment of the promises to Israel and the nations.

God's long awaited rule has arrived in Jesus in an entirely new way. Blessing and judgment are in-fleshed and proliferate in him, as they never had before. What Jesus, empowered by the Spirit, says and does inaugurates the Kingdom of God. The rule of God arrives and is *present* in this fresh and evident manner before a *future* time of final blessing/judgment.

Culmination of what has begun still lies ahead in the complete restoration of creation. To illustrate: when Jesus arrives in his first coming, he brings present manifestations of both God's judgment and his blessing. God's rule has partially arrived. There will come a day in the future however, when Jesus returns and all will have to acknowledge that he is Lord.

The path towards living spirituality now takes on a radical theological and personal illumination as redemption blazes in intensity and the direction for the journey becomes clear. Jesus arrives, announces, and inaugurates the in-breaking rule of God in a unique way through his person and his actions. He is in fact the promised coming one, the one his people had been waiting for to lead them out of exile and into the Kingdom of God.

These key sections of the gospel of Matthew and Jesus' teaching are a true illumination of the path to living spirituality. To follow Jesus is to act, taste, and live upon his word. And this is a matter that concerns the whole person in that it leads to a transformed life and doing the will of the Father.

As Matthew further portrays it, Jesus casts out demons, calms raging storms, releases people from sin, and raises the dead. He is reversing the trajectory of the disfiguring of creation, through appropriating it as his own. These are clear signs that redemption arrives and now begins to work its way to consummation—the restoration of all things. And this illuminates the path for all who are to follow. This is indeed good news for us and the whole of creation.

What is the Kingdom of God?

Having followed the theologically mapped out arrival of redemption, it is important to now focus more particularly on the Kingdom of God. There is an astonishing amount of confusion regarding this particular part of the map. Diverse perspectives circulate today concerning the meaning and relevance of this marker and several of these contribute to spiritual impoverishment. Because of this, it is crucial to have greater clarity on the Kingdom of God if we are to understand the significance of its central place on the journey, and how it directs us and illuminates the path ahead.

In some churches, people currently receive teaching about kingdom life, kingdom theology, kingdom prosperity, and so on. They learn that the Kingdom of God has *already* arrived in its fullness and everything is here for the taking. Other churches teach their congregations that the Kingdom of God is important, but not for this present life. These people are taught that the Kingdom of God has *not yet* arrived, but may do so at some point in the future. Still other churches completely *ignore* the Kingdom of God, attaching little or no importance to it whatsoever. All three of these orientations are unhelpful and contribute to impoverished spirituality because they fail to explain the very basic yet radically mapped description of the Kingdom of God.

We have seen that the Kingdom of God and all that it comprises is absolutely vital to Jesus' person, mission, and ministry. But what are we to understand by God's Kingdom, and *how* is it connected to living Christian spirituality? To start to answer these questions it is best to begin by explaining two things that God's Kingdom is not.

It is not the church

It is often assumed that the Kingdom of God is the church. This is clearly a category mistake. The church is a group of people, not the reign or rule of God. Neither Jesus, nor the first Christian missionaries testified to the church. They proclaimed that Christ was raised and that God had definitively acted to fulfill the promises made long ago. It is important not to misunderstand this point.

As recorded in the gospels, Jesus clearly speaks of his church (Matthew 16:18), but he never equates the church to the Kingdom of God. They are related but also distinct, reminding us here of our broader theological perspective of the character of God.

And we should be careful to maintain this dynamic and positive *tension* as one that is closer to God's truth on this subject as well. If we entirely equate or separate the church and the Kingdom of God, we are moving away from the teaching of Scripture.

It is not narrow

God's rule is not to be limited to Jesus' mission and ministry, death, and resurrection. Why not? If we expand our horizons, it seems fair to say that God has been re-establishing his rule since the catastrophic consequences following the talking serpent's interaction with the images of God in the garden.

Covenant and blessing, law, nation, and prophet, are clearly examples of God's powerful activity in this regard. The point here is that Jesus' incarnation and the accomplishing of his task takes place in a broader context than itself. God's rule is not less than Jesus' incarnated mission and ministry, but it is dynamically more.

While the map of Scripture boldly portrays the *mission* of Jesus as inaugurating the Kingdom of God, and to a lesser degree the church, neither are to be viewed as entirely synonymous with the Kingdom of God. God's Kingdom should not narrowly be seen as the church, nor limited to the mission and ministry, death, and resurrection of Jesus Christ.

It is easier, of course, to say what the Kingdom of God is not rather than to say exactly what it is. When we consider the density of our subject this should not be surprising. Any attempt at a total precision of the magnitude of the Kingdom of God would be dangerous and border on arrogance. Nevertheless, the map of Scripture does offer us a few definite directions about understanding the explosive and powerful character of God's Kingdom.

It is God's rule

God's Kingdom usually refers to the explosive sphere of God's dynamic reign or rule that has *both* already arrived *and* is not yet complete. God's rule is his dynamic act of ruling and all that his rule comprises. Notice that this is an activity—God is ruling and as we follow this rule it directs us to living spirituality. Let's look at it this way. God is engaged in and with the world now. Yet he remains beyond it in order to bring about its full restoration in the future. It is God's activity of blessing and judgment that has, is, and will achieve his consummated rule in history, the cosmos, and our lives.

This dynamic action/rule includes God as Creator, God as love, God as judge, God as the promising covenant-making King of the universe and Israel. His rule is manifest in the Messiah, the outpouring of the Spirit at Pentecost, the church, conversions to Christ Jesus as Lord and Savior today, redemptive activity in the present and ultimately final blessing and judgment on the coming day of Christ.

The Kingdom of God not only dominates Jesus' teaching, it is interlaced throughout the whole of the scriptural map. I think it's best to pay careful attention to it if we are to begin to reverse spiritual impoverishment and to embrace living spirituality.

9

Living Spirituality in the
Already and Not Yet

Now that we have seen the significance of the arrival of the
Messiah and the Kingdom of God for the journey, we are ready to
turn to the task of discovering how the already and not yet character
of the Kingdom of God affects living spirituality. As I pointed out
in the last chapter, many churches today teach that either God's
Kingdom has *already* fully arrived, or that it has *not yet* come at all,
while other churches ignore the Kingdom of God entirely. Each of
these perspectives contributes to spiritual impoverishment at their
own risk and peril. What then are we to make of the *already/not yet*
polarization some churches maintain regarding the Kingdom of
God?

The Kingdom of God, as I mentioned earlier, is to be
understood as both already present and not yet complete. Churches
that polarize, by teaching that the Kingdom of God is either fully
already present *or* not yet present at all, fail to be adequately
representative of the scriptural map and its tensional perspective.
Concerning the Kingdom of God, a *both/and*, already/not yet
tension is closer to biblical truth than an *either/or* resolution. Jesus'

teaching in the gospels affirms this tension, and as Christians we should be living in it.

How does this understanding of the Kingdom of God relate to living spirituality, while countering the either/or extremes that we find in some churches? Let's consider this, starting with an example of over-emphasizing the "already."

The "Already"

We are going to look at Paul's letter to the Corinthians, our 1 Corinthians (5:9 shows that there was a first letter we do not have), which gives us one of the most helpful perspectives on the scriptural map concerning this subject. He writes to a divided, splintered, and fiercely independent community of believers who were struggling with several spirituality issues.

Paul, as an apostle of Christ Jesus to the church of God in Corinth (those sanctified in Christ Jesus), follows his introduction in the first chapter with an *interweaving* of stories. This type of narrating encounter is developed throughout the letter and is a fascinating and dynamic way of letter writing (now would be a good time to open your Bible and to study these chapters).

There is no space here to fully investigate how Paul develops this story. Suffice it to say that the apostle recounts the Corinthians' story (1:4-13), combines it with his own (1:14; 1:26-31), and then highlights God's story as the chief story that the Corinthians are to be living (1:18-25). *Our* stories, as readers, are deeply interconnected with all three of these, and we share much in common with our Corinthian predecessors who first received Paul's letter.

A good deal of ambiguity regarding spirituality existed in Corinth, as is evidenced by the issues raised in Paul's letter. It is clear from various parts of the letter that the underlying problem was that the Corinthians were too "already" oriented in their spirituality (4:8; 7:1-40; 8:1-3). If, as some may have assumed the

Kingdom of God had fully arrived, so had they. Clearly, some Corinthians thought too highly of themselves, supposing they had reached a new plane of life. They were free to do as they pleased, because after all, they were "spiritual" (4:8, 18-19; 5:2). Notions of Christian spirituality in the church today are often as confused as they were in the lives of the Corinthians.

Do you know anyone like this? I have met people who say things that imply, "I can attain such a level of communion with God that I can be totally spiritual in this life." For them, it's as if the body and the physical world are entirely irrelevant to spirituality. All that matters is being fully spiritual now, without the body. Some of the Corinthians may have shared a similar perspective. This over-emphasis on the "already" translated into a fair amount of unspiritual activity and a lack of true wisdom.

The Corinthians raised a matrix of problems that Paul responds to in his letter (sex, marriage, celibacy 7:1-40; spiritual gifts 12-14; the resurrection 15). These issues reveal an underlying dilemma in the Corinthian church. Spiritual enthusiasm proliferated, but it devoured the delicate and balanced tension of the *already* and *not yet*.

A clear expression of this is found in the church's attitude to the body and sexual relations. In the haughty Corinthian slogan, "Everything is permissible for me," Paul adds, "but not everything is beneficial" (6:12). Let's consider this further.

Some men in Corinth were visiting prostitutes (6:12-20), while some women may have been abstaining from sexual relations with their husbands (7:1-7). Both the freedom to engage in sexual relations with prostitutes (liberty) and the freedom to withhold sex from one's husband (asceticism) point to an ambiguous spirituality, particularly in connection to the body.

In the Corinthian church there were those who thought they had *already* arrived and therefore assumed they had license to do with the body whatever they pleased. Perhaps this false scenario sounded something like this: sexual immorality and sex with a prostitute are no problem, because the body is irrelevant to spirituality. Or on the other hand: sex pollutes and denigrates the spiritual through the material interaction of sexual encounter. Stay away from it. The body is only a vehicle to the pollution of the spiritual life. This picture of the body reminds us of those people in the church today who claim the body is useless, because they are already fully spiritual.

Paul will have none of this. Living spirituality, for the apostle, is always an embodied spirituality. In his thinking, there is no dualist notion of a spiritual = good / material = evil. To affirm this anti-dualism, we find Paul puts a repeated emphasis on the body (6:12-20). Because of Christ's resurrection, Christian bodies are part of him. The body is for the Lord. It is the temple of the Holy Spirit. God is to be honored with the body and Christians are to flee sexual immorality, as we have been bought at a price.

After having treated the matter of the body and prostitutes, Paul chooses this appropriate moment to begin his response to the Corinthian letter (7:1). He sets out to respond to the Corinthians' slogan, "It is good for a man not to touch (have sex with) a woman." Notice that in 7:1-16, Paul is addressing people who are already married. He is *not* dealing with the question of whether or not to *get* married until 7:25 and following.

The apostle picks up the issues of sexual immorality (verse 2) and the body (verse 4) from chapter 6, and in verses 2-5 speaks specifically and mutually to married men who may have been visiting prostitutes, and married women who may have been depriving their husbands of sex. Some married women may have assumed that their husbands could have sex, but not with *their* bodies. They believed that the body was part of the material world and therefore evil, and that the sexual act polluted the spiritual. Spirituality and body didn't go together.

The body, however, is neither evil nor irrelevant to living spirituality; it is meant for the Lord. Paul makes it clear that sexual relations in marriage are entirely appropriate and do not falsify this truth. He revolutionizes his cultural norm that the husband possessed his wife's body by envisioning the body as one of mutual belonging, thus bypassing and transforming the notion that it was solely the wife's body that belonged to her husband (7:3-4). This was a shocking disclosure in the apostle's Greco-Roman context and is equally revelatory for living spirituality today.

Paul's rhetoric of equality here points out that in marriage the partners are not free to do what they please with their bodies: neither the man who is visiting prostitutes, nor the woman who is seeking a sexless marriage. Spirituality is an earthly-bodily phenomenon. Liberty and asceticism were two emblems of an overly *already*-focused spirituality that was leading the Corinthians astray. We face similar misunderstandings today. Bodies are worshipped, devalued (liberty), or seen as having nothing to do with the spiritual, which is entirely cut off from the physical world (asceticism).

In contrast, the illuminated pathway points out that living spirituality is not to see the body as irrelevant or evil. The apostle compels married couples to stop defeating each other (7:5), although he concedes there is an appropriate time for abstinence for purposes of prayer, if by mutual consent. Yet sexual relations are part and parcel of a spiritual life when they take place in the right context, and the body is central for living spirituality. Paul concludes the section of verses 1-7 with his preference for singleness, but he is careful to put this in the context of gift, not command.

A Corinthian misunderstanding of the *already* and *not yet* led to significant spiritual confusion with respect to the body and how to live an embodied spirituality in the world. Paul's "but not everything is beneficial" (6:12; 10:23), anchors the Corinthians in the already of the present world, showing that life in it has not yet reached the final goal of God's consummated rule. His numerous correctives to the Corinthians are continually along the lines of the not yet. He consistently seeks to maintain the delicate and balanced tension of a living spirituality between the *already* and *not yet*. In other words, the apostle aims to affirm the present reality of God's rule in the lives of Christians, while at the same time he wants to argue that the future is still ahead. Nothing is complete now, yet what is already true should not be ignored.

It is imperative that we take notice of Paul's perspective, and apply it today to our own notions of spirituality and the body. Churches that teach their congregations that the Kingdom of God has already fully arrived ignore the scriptural map and tend to underplay the significance of the body. For them, being spiritual is divorced from the body and the material world, but such a perspective leads to spiritual impoverishment. In order to reverse this, we are to follow the illuminated path marked out by Scripture (our bodies are the temple of the Holy Spirit), and to live our lives for the sake of the crucified and risen One (with whom our bodies are linked), which means that our spirituality is to be understood as physical, material and embodied.

The "Not Yet"

As the Corinthians, people today seem drawn to extremes that lead to spiritual impoverishment. So it is not surprising that there is also a polarized *not yet* perspective in some churches that contributes to a faulty understanding of the mapping of the Kingdom of God.

Cindy had been a Christian for a number of years. She seemed sad and withdrawn when she arrived at L'Abri. Her unbelieving family accepted her, but not her faith; in fact, they regarded it with some suspicion. She nevertheless attempted to maintain a basic relationship with them in spite of the rejection she sensed. Loyalty was important to Cindy, and it was a trait she hoped others would notice in her. She had worked for a long time for the same company, had attended the same church, and had consistently volunteered with her various groups, but this image of "perfect" loyalty actually disguised something different.

In reality Cindy struggled. She experienced serious bouts of depression, which she attempted to hide by putting on a brave performance. Except for the thought of eventually going to heaven, she found little joy in being a Christian. She often prayed, *Oh God, I hope that someday in the future I'll have intimate contact with you.* In other words, she had an accurate hope for the *not yet*, but the *already* dimension of the reign of God seemed hopelessly inactive in her life.

This absence frequently brought Cindy to tears and sometimes to the verge of a breakdown. She would tell me, "What's the use? I just want to give up." And then, "I have to pick myself up and carry on. But where is God?" Indeed, where was God in the *now* of her life? What could or should she expect the present Christian life to be? Cindy's major problem was the opposite of the Corinthians already focus.

Yes, Cindy was a Christian. The view taught in her church was that the Kingdom of God had not yet arrived, but would do so at some point in the future. She had received little teaching from her church on two central features of the arrival of Kingdom of God: the importance of the present and finished work of Christ for life now, and the significance of the Spirit's work in her daily living. These *already* truths of the Christian life needed exposure and emphasis if Cindy was to begin to move in a new direction.

As we have seen, God's inbreaking rule *was* both a present gift in history and it *will be* an ultimate climax for the future. It had *already* touched Cindy's life in a variety of present ways. She was a Christian—she was born anew; possessed the gift of the Spirit, tasted living water, and was transformed/being transformed through the power of the Spirit already active in her life. These realities were there, but Cindy had not yet grasped the importance of Christ and the Spirit being present in and through her. She needed to act upon these truths for herself in the *now*.

As the parables of Jesus tell us, the Kingdom of God is like a treasure or a priceless pearl that is to be sought here and now.

Nothing is more precious or extravagant. There was no question that God was present in Cindy's life. She was free to live in the joy of being a child of God and the reality that God was working through her, yet she really had not recognized who she already was. Once she began to do this, she would become more aware of the explosive character of living spirituality in her present life.

God's Kingdom, as the rule of God, was a present gift to the world, and this included Cindy. A future hope exists, but a present reality of community with God, based on his revelation and action, is a significant part of life now.

Another way of saying this is that the future has broken into the present, and that this reality touches all of life—how we are to worship God, look at the world, view ourselves, treat our neighbors, do business, evangelize, pray, and so forth. Cindy was not on her own. She did not have to do it all by herself on the basis of her loyalty, commitment, or hard work.

Christians are to live by faith in Christ and in the power of the Spirit and the resurrection—both expressions and activities of God's rule. Cindy began to recognize who she was as saved, released, righteous, and empowered in Christ. She finally understood that the finished work of Christ had a present impact for her life now.

Cindy needed to live actively while trusting God to act through her in this present life. She was called to act on these truths in the power of the Spirit in a daily, even moment-by-moment way: to live in the light of the arrival of the Kingdom of God and all that it comprises in itself. And to live it for her life now.

Churches that teach that the Kingdom of God has not yet arrived banalize the scriptural map and deprive their congregations of the explosive character of God's rule for their present lives. The good news that Jesus preaches is that through his person, mission, ministry, death, and resurrection, the in-breaking reign of God has now arrived in its fullest manifestation. His rule continues to be active today, working its way toward completion in the future restoration of heaven and earth.

As disciples of Jesus, we are called to be involved as active participants in what we believe. We are to embrace God and the kingdom. If we are to reverse impoverished spirituality, it is imperative to be acting in the light that God's reign is central to living spirituality. It charts out our directions into all areas of life both now and as we look forward to the future day of Christ when every knee will bow to his authority. Living in the *already* and *not yet* tension of the present and future of the Kingdom of God incorporates a call to live as if we are in God's very presence now.

Living spirituality is living in this tension. Cindy found this priceless treasure and as she embraced it for herself, her life began to change in dramatic ways. She too saw herself in the light of the arrival of the Kingdom of God and in some sense, as already raised with Christ, a citizen of heaven, and a new self now in the present.

Living the Tension

The perspective that God's Kingdom has already arrived and is not yet complete is marked by a tension. Living *tensions* will proliferate in this context, but it is imperative to realize that tension is not to be understood as a flaw in our spirituality. Tension is not a negative thing. It is not something we should attempt to disguise or destroy.

Christians devote a tremendous amount of time and energy attempting to exorcise tension. In my view, this is a utopian misinterpretation of living spirituality and not the direction God has for us. To be in tension is to be in-between. And being in-between corresponds to the theological marker of the Kingdom of God, to life in the world, and to who we are as creatures of God.

Given the contours of what we have discussed, this tension is positive and appropriate. Its explicit marker on the map is the character of the Kingdom of God, but tension is also true for the whole of living spirituality; we live in the sufficiency of the *already* and await the completion of the *not yet.*

In this context, it is important to see the *already* part of spirituality representing God's work in the world and in our own lives at the present time. In spite of the truth that not everything is resolved now, we have great hope rooted deeply in God's truth and living in community with him and his people. God's faithful present is *already* ours as we patiently await the culmination of his faithful *not yet.*

10

The Death and Resurrection of Christ: Their Meaning for Living Spirituality

The journey continues. We look up to get a visual of the terrain before consulting the map of Scripture again. Now that we have spent time walking through a theological-spiritual understanding of the Creator, creation, covenant, the arrival of the Messiah and the Kingdom of God, and the already and not yet, we will further proceed on the journey by passing through the astonishing events of the death and resurrection of Christ.

We face the danger of severe spiritual impoverishment when we lack a biblical understanding of the death and resurrection of Christ. It is crucial to be aware that these events, mapped out in Scripture, are a vital part of our theology and living spirituality. They take place within the arrival of God's Kingdom and the already and not yet as they apply to the Christian life.

The pivotal place of the death of Christ is generally ignored in popularized versions of spirituality today, which all too often mirror the cultural pursuits of health, wealth, and positive thinking. After all, who wants anything to do with a dead Messiah? How could such a death have any benefits for ME?

Contemporary Christian thought also puts a tremendous emphasis on ME in terms of deciding the value and relevance of Christ's death. My needs and problems become central. Unfortunately, this shallow perspective is widespread. According to some Christians, all that counts is: what's in this for ME?

Our obsession with ME subverts the truth that the death of Christ is a key event in the establishment of God's rule. Why did Christ die? Christians often respond, "He died for ME and my sins." While this is astonishingly true, there is a caveat—Christ died for far more than that. The whole of God's reign is at stake in Christ's death as he takes the covenant curses upon himself. The Kingdom of God has burst on the scene, and the death of Christ is first and foremost about inaugurating this rule. Christ's death is *not about less* than ME and my sins, but it is always superabundantly *about so much more*—God's establishing his rule and restoring all things. And that is what we miss.

When I put myself, ME, at the center, the death of Christ and living spirituality are considerably impoverished. There is a place for me, which I will develop more fully later, but it is important to say no to ME being at the center. This involves a real battle—the battle with sin. Life and death are at stake. And if we choose to center on ME, we are facing the significant danger of embracing forms of spiritual impoverishment—notably, idolatry and self-deception.

Christians are called to live otherwise: for the Other and others. We are not called to constantly focus on ourselves. The scriptural mapping speaks of loving others and serving them. It speaks of evangelism, social action, and putting others before ourselves as illuminating the true path toward living spirituality. And Christ is the prime example in that he became human and lived and died for others.

Christ's death, however, is not the end of the matter. God's rule is further manifested in his resurrection. He was raised from the dead and is now present with God and interceding on behalf of his people. In much popular theology/spirituality today, the resurrection of Christ is reduced to the experience of Christ being raised in one's heart.

Not only does such a perspective undervalue the map and downplay a real theological referent for the heart, it leads back to the false referent of ME—a form of dying spirituality. When there is no personal external referent for spirituality, notably the Infinite God, everything rests on ME and my experience or feeling of Christ being raised. Such a ME emphasis results in a naturalistic, *humanistic* referent stripped of any godly supernatural reality and power.

If Christ is merely raised in our hearts, our faith is in vain and we have lost our view of the origin and ultimate source of spirituality, which first belongs to Father, Son and Spirit, before it becomes our own. If we succumb to this impoverished ME version of spirituality, we fail to be spiritual and become hypocritical—hypocrites because we seek to make that which does not first belong to us our possession.

Living spirituality, in contrast, is far from centering on ME or having nothing to do with a real death and resurrection. The death of Christ, the supreme death, is the death that makes new life possible. Christ's death and resurrection becomes, and forever will be the threshold to redemption and community with God.

In the New Testament letter to the Romans, the apostle Paul rivets attention on these very issues. How and why does the death and resurrection of Christ make a difference to our spirituality and identity? Where, as Christians, do we find ourselves and who are we?

To answer these questions, we are going to spend some time with Romans 6, which you will find included below. This key chapter, an integral part of the scriptural map, helps illuminate the path into living spirituality.

Paul sets the course in chapter 5. Here, he precisely draws out the meaning of Christ's death and resurrection for us, while pointing out how to live in relationship to the law, sin, grace, life and death. The impact of the apostle's previous sketch of salvation history is rooted in a radical difference—an orientation of belonging to either Adam or Christ. Since grace is supposed to have overpowered sin, the burning question now becomes: if grace increases when sin increases, why not live a life of sin?

Some Roman Christians may have been accusing Paul of preaching that there was nothing wrong with a sin-based spirituality if it produces grace. The apostle is far from talking theory here. He stresses the double-edged truth that grace reigns and sin matters. He wants to know if Christians realize who they are in Christ. And he is deeply concerned about how they are to live spiritual lives in the light of God's superabundant grace.

Romans 6:1-11: Dying and Living with Christ

(1) What shall we then say? Shall we go on sinning so that grace may increase? (2) By no means! We died to sin; how can we live in it any longer? (3) Or don't you know that all of us who have been baptized into Christ Jesus were baptized into his death? (4) We were therefore buried with him through baptism into death in order that, just as Christ was raised from the dead through the glory of the Father, we may too live a new life.

(5) For if we have been united with him like this in his death, we will certainly also be united with him in his resurrection. (6) For we know that our old self was crucified with him so that the body of sin might be rendered powerless, that we should no longer be slaves to sin (7) because anyone who has died has been freed from sin. (8) Now if we have died with Christ, we believe that we will also live with him. (9) For we know that Christ, being raised from the dead, will never die again; death no longer has dominion over him. (10) The death he died, he died to sin, once for all; but the life he lives he lives to God. (11) In the same way, count yourselves dead to sin but alive to God in Christ Jesus.

Paul anticipates his audience's response to what he has written in the previous chapter and poses two questions in the first verse:

1. What then shall we say?
2. Does a superabundance of grace encourage sin?

What shall we say indeed? Paul writes that grace—not the law—is the only true solution to sin. If this is the case, how are we to situate ourselves with respect to this chapter and living spirituality?

Emphatically, in verse 2, the apostle rejects the idea that a Christian should sin for grace to increase. "By no means," he writes, "we died to sin." He then asks the rhetorical question, "How can we live in it any longer?"

Indeed, an excellent question to contemplate. How can a Christian live in sin? If we are to find an answer we must first ask another question: what is Paul likely to mean by "living in sin"?

His thought seems to relate to the aim of avoiding sin in our lives. Living in sin refers then to living a life oriented to sin. That is, it is following representative Adam, rather than representative Christ. Ultimately, we either follow and are oriented to *death* in Adam or to *life* in Christ. But why is this the case and where is it all going?

I suggest something like this—God's act of superabundant grace in Christ transfers Christians from the reign of sin to the reign of grace. In the light of this truth, rooted in the work of Christ, there is no reciprocity between them. Sin and grace are not to be viewed or lived as equals. And because the reign of sin is already broken, the apostle can write: "How can we who died to sin go on living in it?"

This radical affirmation, on the basis of what God has superabundantly done, encourages us to recognize who we are as believers. We are no longer to incessantly promote and continually choose sin in our lives. We will sin, of course, but this is not our

83

orientation. A new orientation and a new life are established by faith in Christ. New ways of being, seeing, and living are the outcome of an encounter with the *crucified* and *risen* One, and the transforming power of the Spirit that Paul will focus more intently on in chapter 8.

Through God's grace, the dominion of sin in our lives is already shattered, although it is not yet completely destroyed. As we look forward to the latter, it is Christ himself, his death on the cross and his resurrection, which is the mediation point between grace and sin. The cross and resurrection of Christ are the place we gravitate toward and are grafted into when it comes to living spirituality.

In verse 3, "Do you not know . . ." implies at least some common recognition between the apostle and his audience concerning what he is writing. He wants his readers to be more aware of what has taken place on their behalf, and who they are in light of their participation in that gift.

Baptism

Paul next goes on to baptism. Baptism is used here as a mediatory (as opposed to a restrictive) term for incorporation into Christ Jesus. This may be new to us and somewhat difficult to understand, but it pictures Christ as a corporate figure. He is not some great, indefinable mass that we seek to be joined with, as in some nature or new age spiritualities. Christ is the incarnated, personal-historic Son of God who is Lord, and who in his death and resurrection is able to incorporate those who follow him.

When we become Christians it is important to note that it is not sin that dies, but it is we *ourselves who die*. Through this death, we are joined to or *baptized* into Christ's death. Only because Christ is now the risen corporate One can believers be referred to as those baptized into his death, a death which represents their own.

Reflect for a moment again on both relation and distinction. How does this play itself out in this context? Living in community with God as followers of Christ means we are related to Christ, incorporated into Christ, yet we do not become Christ. Christians and Christ remain distinct. Christ is the unique, divine Savior, while Christians are not and never will be who he is. We have true union with Christ, but are not Christ.

Paul's explanation and continuation in verse 4 expresses the further significance of union with Christ. Remember that baptism is a metaphor for our initiation into his death. Because of this alliance, which Paul refers to as being *buried with him*, our own death is thereby configured and positioned in the death of Christ. The apostle then can exhort: so that just as Christ was raised, Christians too might *walk* in a newness of life.

To walk in the newness of life is dramatically compared to the resurrection of Christ and is a metaphor for directing the whole of one's life toward the goal. And it is because Christ is raised that his followers are released, empowered, and challenged to live new lives in their present circumstances.

This picture is similar to the striking, even astonishing verses in Ephesians 1:15-23. The paragraph there is a richly textured treasure we cannot fully develop here. I just want to point out that this passage compares the power at work in the lives of those who believe to the power that God exerted when he raised Christ from the dead and seated him above all rule, authority, power, and dominion. Indeed, a bold and pretty amazing *power* statement.

The *power* orientation for Christians is now toward Christ, not Adam; toward grace, not sin. Life and how to live it are deliberately centered on a new understanding of the person and work of Christ. Let's be aware of that power at work, be aware of who we are, and be aware of who we will become as we follow in the footsteps of Christ.

Back in Romans, the next verse makes explicit both our orientation and unity. In verse 5 the apostle first affirms, "*For* if we have been united in the likeness of his death" (in a death like Christ's). Paul is not writing about biological-physical death, but rather of death to the old ways of living in and choosing sin. For the believer, the possibility of living a new way takes place through Christ's death, which overcame the hierarchical and devastating power of sin and death.

It is important to note that Paul uses the perfect tense in, "we have been united." A perfect tense speaks of a past unity that is ongoing and relevant for the present. The point is: the effects of the crucified One's death are a present reality for Christians in every age.

If believers have been and are still being united in the likeness of Christ's death, the apostle points out (verse 5b) that "we will certainly also be united with him in his resurrection." This time, "we will be united" is a future tense pointing to the goal of a full transformation of our bodies.

However, we should remember at this juncture the empowerment that Christ's resurrection has provided us with (back in verse 4) in our present context. Walking in the newness of life works its way back from future to present, and is a reality that is to be embraced and lived now. But how are we to envision this?

The apostle crystallizes the meaning of the Christian's death with Christ in verses 6-7. He writes of the old self, the person as related to Adam. This person undergoes a theologically changed relationship—old to new—in relation to the Adam-Christ orientation. This person is crucified with Christ so that the body of sin (not just physical but relational—the whole person) might be made powerless. Why? Notably, so that Christians should no longer serve sin.

The use of "body," in this context refers to more than physical flesh. We should understand it as a reference to our whole person in our situation and relation to the world. A relational-positional change has taken place in our lives that orients itself toward rendering all sin powerless, whether it is physical or otherwise. The result of this is that we no longer serve sin. How is this possible? The key that unlocks the mystery is found in the reality that those who are united in community with Christ and his resurrection are empowered to live in a new way.

The explanatory "because" of verse 7 puts together death (crucified with Christ) and sin (no longer serving sin). Paul's general point is that death breaks the hold of sin over a person. We are no longer *possessed* by sin in that there is unity, both a positional and relational unity, in community with Christ.

In verses 8-11, Paul repeats and expands on some of what we have just looked at. If we died with Christ, we also believe that we will live with him. This belief of living with Christ is related to knowledge concerning his resurrection, as his resurrection defeats death, resulting in illuminating a new path to life for all who follow. Christ's resurrection then graphically anticipates our own.

Paul writes that Christ "died to sin once for all." He was subject to the power of sin and he identifies with those under the dominion of sin and death. And because of this identification and his resurrection, we too now have a resurrected life—life we are to live, as Christ does—to and for God.

As the radical break between representatives (Adam-Christ) has now come to pass, the apostle can declare that death no longer reigns. God's grace, in Christ, has reached its fullest and most complete manifestation prior to final judgment and the ultimate consummation of God's Kingdom. Though the death and resurrection of Christ was a one time historical event, he now lives a never-ending life (present continuous tense) to and for God. This shows us that the risen One's post-resurrection power over death and sin is undefeatable. And that the seemingly unquenchable thirst of death has been drowned by the blood of Christ, which leads to never-ending life for all who have died with him.

The Constant Reminder

Verse 11 provides us with the application of this for the believing community. Paul uses a present imperative here to send us back to verses 1-2: "In the same way, count yourselves dead to sin, but alive to God in Christ Jesus." Believers then, are to *continually* (as the present imperative affirms) count themselves dead to sin as the first part of the imperative states. Remember that God has declared sinners holy and righteous through the work of Christ. This does not mean that a Christian never sins; again, the point is chiefly one of orientation.

Those who are declared righteous by God through faith in Christ must continually—as in daily, even moment by moment—reckon themselves dead to sin. Sin is not dead, but the believer is dead to it. How? Why? Their own deaths, through participation in Christ's death (as we have seen in verse 4), have brought release from the powerful and dominating *reign* of sin in their lives.

If this is the case, then Christians have a responsibility in living spirituality. They are to embody and embrace a life lived toward God, while counting themselves free from the *reign* of sin. The apostle will explain this further as he goes on to affirm the new orientation.

The second part of Paul's imperative shows that Christians are "alive to God in Christ Jesus." As the resurrected One lives to God (verse 10), we too are to realize that our lives are oriented to God, which equates life. We are alive to God and in union with Christ through his resurrection.

The results of this are staggering—not a passive static state, but the reality of a dynamic community with the living God and his people. Following in the footsteps of the crucified and risen One means Christians are alive to God in Christ in the present life. Being in community with God and each other makes for a compelling and magisterial case for living spirituality, reversing the impoverishment of ME at the center, and bringing forth the reality of being *alive* to God in who we are and in what we say and do. And this saying and doing is for the sake of Christ, and to the glory of God.

Romans 6:12-14: Indicatives and Imperatives

(12) Therefore, do not let sin exercise dominion in your mortal body, so that you obey its evil desires. (13) Do not offer the parts of your body to sin, as instruments of wickedness, but rather offer yourselves to God, as those who have been brought from death to life; and offer the parts of your body to him as instruments of righteousness. (14) For sin shall not be your master, because you are not under law, but under grace.

Now we come to a transition. That means this very short section of verses 12-14 is related to verses 1-11 and also to 15-23. In these three verses, Paul looks both backward and forward, and continues with more imperatives and an indicative in verse 14.

When we think of who we are as Christians, it is important to not forget the astounding statements of verses 1-11. Look at it this way. True holiness only comes from our union with Christ. None of us achieve holiness on our own, but at the same time we must recognize our own responsibility to accept God's work on our behalf. Often, we readily do this in justification, but we tend to minimize his work when it comes to a moment-by-moment living spirituality.

I would argue that the apostle does not aim to resolve our tension here, but to affirm us in it. And this is how: we have *already* died with Christ, but we are *not yet* physically raised with him. We are dead to sin, but we must make an effort to not let it reign in our mortal bodies. Tension continues to be a reality of living spirituality. Such a tension, as we recall from the scriptural mapping is not a negative, but rather is a key component of the true spiritual life.

What Paul goes on to write in verse 12 referring to "mortal bodies" is no accident. Though it is true that Christians are no longer part of the "body of sin," they still have mortal bodies. We can say that until the whole person is fully redeemed, including the body, the person remains subject to this world and its influences. The apostle uses "mortal body" here to remind us that our battle with evil desires and sin continues, because the whole person is engaged in this present age.

The Present Tense of Sin

As we are still living in this age, we must be aware that sin is always present tense. Sin persistently attempts to rule over us and establish its supremacy. Paul insists that because of what God has done in Christ, and because of the believer's community with both Christ's person and his work, we are not to let sin rule over us. We are not to succumb to its influence and control.

Yes, as believers we are still in this world and are subject to the power of sin, but sin no longer has the power to reign over and dominate us. Paul argues that because of God's grace the believer's orientation is now directed toward God, rather than away from God.

Verse 13 goes on to give a more specific imperative. "Do not turn over [present tense, as in daily] your natural capacities to sin as weapons [power-authority] of unrighteousness [all that is against God]." Though the risk of doing so remains with us until the end of our lives, the apostle argues that we are to turn ourselves over to God because we have been brought from death to life.

In this context, we are reminded of our aliveness in God (verse 11). Paul's imperative carries with it no pretense, no psychological manipulation, and no stoic asceticism. Why is this the case? In his view, Christ's resurrection has changed the course of history by mapping out the pathway to life—we are alive to God.

If God's act of superabundant grace in history, the journey and in our own journey is true, then we are to turn over all of who we are (natural capacities) to God as weapons of righteousness. How? By re-affirming God's gracious act of further establishing his rule through Christ's death and resurrection, and by surrendering ourselves to God. Living in love, for God and each other, serves the cause of righteousness and promotes living spirituality.

A Promise in Action

In verse 14 after the imperatives, Paul confirms this very reality with an indicative. When one becomes a Christian there is a transfer of lordship—a transfer of representatives and representation—that has already taken place.

The apostle uses the future tense to express the function of a promise in action: "For sin shall not be lord over you." Why a promise in action? First, the promise is inaugurated because of Christ's work. Second, it is inaugurated because of a believer's union with the *crucified* and *risen* One.

This promise will ultimately be fulfilled when believers see Christ face to face, but it is already moving toward such fulfillment in relationship to the imperatives in verses 12-13. "For sin shall not be lord over you." A Christian response should be, "No, it won't." And furthermore, "Why is this the case?"

The truth of the matter is that if we are aligned with the *crucified* and *risen* One who is our representative, our whole orientation is refigured in the direction of community with God and the life God offers. This cannot be accomplished through a simple act of discipline on our part. Discipline alone could never take us here. Rather, God has empowered us through his grace, through the gift of righteousness, and through a union with Christ to live in a new way. This recognition carries with it a new allegiance; not to sin, but to God. It is this power that operates in living spirituality and enables a Christian to live life toward God.

The enactment of this transfer of lordship, of representatives, is working its way to completion in the lives of Christians now, even in a moment-by-moment way. Just because it will only be complete in the future does not mean it is irrelevant or insignificant for living our present lives. We are *alive* to God in Christ.

In moving to the affirmation of this promise in part b of verse 14, the apostle shifts to the present tense. The reason that sin shall not be lord over a believer is because a believer is not under law, but under grace.

As we have seen previously in regard to sin and grace, both law and grace are presented as powers that a Christian is subject to. Powers either under the old regime and representative, Adam: or under the new and representative, Christ. Followers of the crucified and risen One find their rest and solace under this new regime. But ever alert to our humanity, Paul clearly and carefully points out this does not give us permission to become complacent. Let's solidify our understanding of the role of sin and grace in a believer's life.

Romans 6:15-23: Freed from Sin

(15) What then? Shall we sin because we are not under law, but under grace? (16) By no means! Don't you know that when you offer yourselves to someone as obedient slaves, you are slaves to the one whom you obey, whether you are slaves to sin, which leads to death, or of obedience, which leads to righteousness? (17) But thanks be to God that, though you used to be slaves to sin, you wholeheartedly obeyed the form of teaching to which you were entrusted. (18) You have been set free from sin and have become slaves of righteousness.

(19) I put this in human terms because you are weak in your natural selves. Just as you used to offer the parts of your body in slavery to impurity and ever increasing wickedness, so now offer them in slavery to righteousness for sanctification. (20) When you were slaves to sin, you were free from the control of righteousness. (21) What benefit did you reap at that time from the things that you are now ashamed of? Those things result in death! (22) But now

that you have been set free from sin and have become slaves to God, the benefit you reap leads to sanctification, and the result is eternal life. (23) For the wages of sin is death, but the gift of God is eternal life in Christ Jesus our Lord.

You can see a fair amount of similarity between these verses and 1-14. Verse 15 picks up verse 1 with another rhetorical question. The difference this time is that verse 15 relates not to the question of sinning so that grace might increase, but to sinning because of grace.

Paul, again, anticipates the reaction of his reader, a legalist or a legalistic Christian. It would have been and still is a shocking thought to be lawless—not regulated by the law. The reader's response may run something like this:

Listen Paul, if we are under grace and not law, then we are free to sin. It doesn't really matter.

The apostle responds to the question in the same way as he did in verse 1: "By no means." There is something more important than the law, namely, community with the living God through faith in Christ.

Are we Free to Sin?

Verse 16 assumes Paul's readers have a degree of familiarity with the scenario he presents. He argues that in the act of turning oneself over to someone in obedience, you are a slave to the one you obey. What the apostle has in mind is not a legal status, but a life experience.

He clarifies his point as the verse proceeds. Either we are slaves to sin (possessed by sin) which leads to death, or we are slaves to obedience (possessed by obedience) which leads to righteousness. Paul probably contrasts obedience with sin here to avoid the accusation of preaching an obedience-free gospel—cheap grace. No, he argues, there is a significant place for obedience in the Christian life, but to whom and to what is the more pertinent question.

The Transfer of Masters

The transfer of masters the apostle has in mind takes place in verses 17-18. He gives thanks to God that his readers are no longer slaves to sin; they have now obeyed the authoritative teaching under which they have been placed. And most importantly, they obeyed internally, from the heart—not from an external, ritualized obedience to the law.

The heart is a key component of living spirituality. God wants our hearts, not merely some exterior performance that relegates spirituality to a lifeless mantra. His desire is for the whole of who we are to be in community with him and to follow the map that he has so graciously given. When we choose to follow it, we are guided into the life he has for us—a life that is to be lived from the heart.

Even though Christians are no longer under Mosaic law, they are still under grace. And grace does not mean formlessness, just *making it up as we go along*, which leads to impoverished spirituality. Grace does not mean that there is no pattern or any authoritative teaching that we should model our lives after. We have the prime example: the *crucified* and *risen* One who is the very fullness of God and his grace.

The life, death, and resurrection of Christ are the imprint for redemption, which stamps itself upon us in living spirituality. These events are the key markers on the map for our journey and they open up the path to life. To obey from the heart is to live a new life, understanding the double-edged truth that grace reigns *and* that sin is no longer our master.

In verse 18 we see how this plays out. When we obey the gospel teachings from the heart under God's grace, we are released from sin and its enslaving power and at the same time, we are enslaved to the greater power of righteousness.

Paul then establishes a contrast in verse 19. Just as his readers used to turn themselves over to be slaves to sinful acts and behavior—to the vicious cycle of unrighteousness—so now, as Christians, they have an equally vigilant goal to turn themselves over to righteousness by doing what is right before God, which leads to holy living.

Remember though, this imperative relates back to the indicative of God's work for believers in Christ and the union that they have with him as a result of this. We are no longer enslaved to unrighteousness, which leads us toward sin and death, but to righteousness, which leads us toward grace and life.

The contrasts continue in verses 20-23. When we are possessed by sin, we are free from the power of righteousness. But the result of such a freedom is death. So what benefit, the apostle asks in verse 21, is there in sin? This is a shocking question. And the answer is nothing, because it results in death. All that is sinful fails to contribute to life in any living way. Whatever its pretensions, or our assumptions, it offers us zero, brings us no real advantages, and leaves us aimlessly wandering away from the path to life. The result of the things we are now ashamed of is death. But now we are freed from sin and slaves to God, which results in sanctification and everlasting life.

Far from embracing the mentality that sin might increase grace if we promote sin, Paul radically argues that we have been set free from sin. We belong to God. The transfer has taken place. And the results of such a transfer bring forth community with God, living spirituality, and life now and ultimately in the age to come. This in turn leads us to the final contrast in verse 23. Which orientation are we to embrace as our own—the gift or sin? Sin only leads to death, while the free gift of God leads to life in Christ Jesus our Lord. *Consider this attentively and thoughtfully.*

What Romans 6 Teaches Us

Romans 6 takes us far from the impoverished notions of spirituality in the ME-centered culture we are part of, and reorients us with a radically counter-cultural emphasis centering on the crucified and risen One. And it is here, as followers of this One, that we are truly rebels who stand against the mirage of the status quo of ME, and rest in community with God, through Christ. It is he, not we, who has rightful place at the center of living spirituality.

Christ is not, in Paul's portrayal, a figure that can be reduced to being raised merely in our hearts. He is truly the Messiah, the *crucified* and *risen* One, who inaugurates the Kingdom of God, and lived, died, and was raised in history. There is nothing that will have greater significance in the unfolding rule of God until we reach the end, culminating in God's final restoration of all things.

Christians, Paul made evident, have a new orientation. They are moving toward Christ—not Adam—as Christ is now our representative. Having died to sin, we are alive to God. As a result of being alive to God, we receive the gift of community with God, which in turn enables us to be engaged in living and true spirituality, expressing love and grace toward others. Being in community with God offers us the opportunity to be in authentic community with each other, and to live this authenticity out into the world for the sake of Christ.

In living this spirituality, Christians need to take time to nourish real relationships and to build communities that represent a shared life; a life together. We should learn to fast and feast as one, share books and stories jointly, listen to each other in attentive and caring ways, support and encourage, and be willing to accept and offer loving critique where necessary.

Real relationships and shared lives, with Christ at the center and empowered by the Spirit, will lead to transformation into the image of Christ. We will experience new ways of seeing, being, speaking, and acting. And this type of transformation, lived in the Christian community, is also capable of being lived out in the world to the glory of God.

11

Justification and Sanctification

We have spent considerable time in Romans 6. I hope that the exposition helped reveal the radical theological importance of the death and resurrection of Christ for our journey. As Christians we have a new representative and a new orientation, and we are to embrace this gift and live it as our own. Romans 6 also gave us the correct perspective from which to view ourselves, to newly understand who we are, and how and why the finished work of Christ makes a difference for the whole of life.

In the next chapters, as we continue further on the journey following the map and the guide, we are going to explore several other crucial issues for understanding living spirituality. In this chapter, we will focus on the relevance of justification and sanctification. These two theological markers face a number of forms of impoverishment today. I intend to first briefly sketch out two impoverished views of justification and then offer alternatives, before going on to address a number of impoverished views of sanctification and then suggest alternatives to reverse these.

Jason's Story

The first impoverished view of justification is that *being* a Christian is a process that will eventually become a finished work. When Jason came to L'Abri he was not a follower of Jesus. He had been burned by trite and superficial notions of conversion, which caused him to become highly suspicious. One of the last things on his mind was to draw any distinct conclusions.

Jason believed that he was on the way to someday being justified. Allergic to trusting anything or anyone, or so he said, Jason assumed that such things could be viewed as "in process." For him this resulted in a perpetual postponement of trusting God, of making a decision on conversion, or of being committed to Christ. Eventually, Jason thought, he might become a justified believer in Christ, but that was entirely dependent on how the process developed and where it took him.

Soon after he arrived in the community, Jason became aware that he indeed trusted something: notably himself. His views of process and his own suspicions were what he saw as directing his life. Did they merit this authoritative position? Were they worth what he thought they were? Jason discovered that suspicion is never a first-order discourse, because it is always preceded by trust—perhaps a trust that was broken, but trust nevertheless. What explains this priority of trust? Trust comes first because we are images of God. For Jason, as for us all, trust is already there and directs our lives. We may falsely presume that we are thoroughly and exclusively suspicious, yet the bottom line is that we are always trusting that our suspicions are accurate. There is no way to escape trust.

This is an important issue for justification since it relates to both the wonder and ruin of being human. Jason had to deal with this and think it through carefully. Why was he, a human being, incapable of escaping the fact that trust came first? He had to consider that God, in his grace, has wonderfully made us this way. Yet we are broken—wondrous ruins. It is not as if we don't trust, we actually do. Our problem is that we trust in the wrong things. Instead of trusting God we often blindly trust ourselves, our suspicions, or some process that may eventually lead us to justification.

The scriptural map, as we will see, clarifies that justification takes place once for all on the basis of the finished work of Christ. There is no more or less when it comes to justification. Either we are justified in Christ, or we are not.

Jason needed to trust in God. Trusting God, and in his provision for the release of our sins on account of Christ, is to *be* justified. To *be* justified before God, to be declared righteous in his eyes does not end in process. There may be a process of *becoming* justified, but this always should be viewed as leading to a decision of accepting Christ and being justified. Otherwise, becoming too often functions as an excuse for not being. We continually delay commitment for some elusive and opaque notion that this may happen someday.

Like Jason, we all need to understand this *being* justified as taking place within a sphere of time. In that time, we stop *becoming* justified to *be* justified on the basis of accepting the finished work of Christ. The goal is *being* justified today. This is not an ongoing process that is *becoming* true over an undefined period without decision and commitment, or that may become true someday in spite of them. Instead it is an active bowing before God today, this day, and accepting his offer of grace in Christ.

Caroline's Story

The second impoverished notion of justification is connected to the legalistic and desperate sense that we have to *do* something to merit being justified. Caroline was always busy in a flurry of activity. She *did*, and *did* to the point of exhaustion. In our community context of life together in L'Abri this became unmistakably evident. What was behind it all? Why the stress and anxiety to *do* and *do*?

Caroline thought she needed to *do* so that God would declare her righteous. This required her constant performance for others and for God. She learned how to make herself appear to be a strong Christian, but she came to realize she was wearing a mask. One of her key issues, she eventually recounted, was that she wanted God to change her. Yet, what this really amounted to was that she thought God should hide her sin—not because she was sorry for it, but so that she might look better before others and not be rejected.

A powerful legalism flourished in Caroline's life. Everything stood or fell on how well she followed the laws. If she thought she had done enough in a day, then she was entitled to see herself as worthy and meriting justification. If she didn't measure up to her codes and regimes, or those that others had imposed upon her, she viewed herself as condemned. This vicious circle led her to repeated defeat and perplexity, with seemingly no way out of the maze.

Caroline needed to become aware of an entirely new way of seeing things. It was a revelation to her to understand that Christ did for her what she could never do for herself. And that she had misconstrued what she was asking God to do for her. God is not out to hide our sin, but to expose it. In Christ, God had already done everything necessary for her justification. If she confessed Christ as Messiah, she was justified.

To be justified by God, to be declared righteous, was the gift she could accept with the empty hands of faith. Caroline had been so caught up in a *doing* mentality that she missed the essential truth of justification as a gift. There is, of course, a place for a *being*-and-*doing* connection, but Caroline had put *doing* before *being*. She came to realize that *doing* is crucial, but that it comes out of *being* justified.

These two stories of impoverished views of justification reveal something of the current misunderstanding today and the need for alternatives to reverse this. If we are to reverse spiritual impoverishment on this important issue, it is essential to have a clear perception of the map.

Justification

Justification highlights God's covenant intention to release us from sin through the finished work of Christ. To be living spirituality, as I have already pointed out, we must first be disciples of Jesus. This is the way everyone must come to the living God. We were separated from community with him as a result of sin. Only the gift of the blood of Christ can release us from guilt and sin and transfer us back into community with God. And only that gift can illuminate the path from distorted creation and spiritual impoverishment, to living spirituality.

In consultation with the map, the course set out for us is found in Romans 3:21-26:

(21) But now a righteousness from God, apart from the law, has been made known, to which the Law and the Prophets testify. (22) This righteousness from God comes through faith in Jesus Christ to all who believe. There is no difference, (23) for all have sinned and fall short of the glory of God, (24) and are justified freely by his grace through the redemption that came by Christ Jesus. (25) God presented him as a sacrifice of atonement, through faith in his blood. (26) He did this to demonstrate his justice, because in his forbearance he had left the sins committed beforehand unpunished—he did it to demonstrate his justice at the present time, so as to be just and the one who justifies those who have faith in Jesus.

Here we see that God's righteousness has been revealed. The prophets and law attest to it. All who believe and have faith in Jesus Christ will receive God's righteousness.

This brings us to the heart of Paul's letter to Rome. In the previous section (3:1-20), the apostle has already written that no one is righteous before God, and no one will be justified by observing the law. These, of course, were two of the pillars of the Jewish race: righteousness and the law.

The section begins with "but now," introducing a contrast with the previous discussion, and highlighting the transition from the age of law to the age of Christ (see the clear links with 1:17). In other words, this new revelation from God has already taken place in the redemptive events of Christ's death and resurrection. In Christ, God has intervened in a new way to make provision for being justified, for being declared righteous.

Paul points out that this *now* righteousness, revealed from God, is apart from the law. "Apart from the law" seems to signify that it is apart from the law as misunderstood from a Jewish perspective. That is, the assumption that having the law led to a favored status with God, irrespective of the Messiah. Thus, when the possession of the law is understood as a badge of righteousness, "apart from the law" is essential for understanding what God was doing.

On the other hand, notice the apostle argues, that both the law and the prophets testify repeatedly to this newly revealed righteousness. The aim of the law and prophets was not to be a Jewish badge, but to reveal God's plan to redeem humanity through Israel's Messiah. What God was up to in the Messiah was a fulfillment, even culmination of that plan.

If we see "apart from the law" and the "law and prophets testifying," as both important, we have a relation and a distinction here concerning the law. Everything turns on how the law is viewed and understood.

Moving on through Romans 3, Paul points out that justification comes through the redemptive and the finished work of Christ. For us, it is crucial to then appropriate this in faith. Jason needed to come to believe—to *be* a believer and to have faith in Christ in

103

order to *be* justified, not merely belong to a lifelong process of *becoming* justified.

This perspective brings us back to relation and distinction. Notice the relevance of this configuration for an understanding of faith. We need to be clear on this one: justification is not faith. Faith is related to justification, but it is also distinct from it. Why? The main reason is that Jesus Christ, the Messiah, is both the righteousness from God and a Christian's righteousness before God, through faith.

Our faith is not the referent for itself. Revealed righteousness exists whether we have faith or not, as it is anchored in the finished work of Christ. Faith, in this context, as Caroline came to see, is bowing and simply saying "yes" to God with empty hands. It is the way of appropriating and receiving the finished work of Christ as a gift for oneself: *being* justified.

The direction of Paul's text then shifts. He moves from *receiving* righteousness freely (by God's grace, as a gift, and through the ransom in Christ) to the fact that it is solely God's *initiative* that makes this possible. Notice that this speaks of God fulfilling the covenant and doing the reconciling for sinners, not sinners doing the reconciling for God. If we think we can reconcile ourselves to God, we have misunderstood God's initiative and the trajectory of justification as a part of salvation.

The aim of this brief introduction to justification is to highlight that it is not possible to be more or less justified. The finished work of Christ for justification is a completed and unlimited gift. As a result, there is no condemnation for those who follow him on the path to life. Paul develops this perspective later in Romans and clearly points out that God sent his own Son in flesh, and condemned sin in flesh, so that the law might be fulfilled in us who live our lives by the Spirit and not by the flesh. When we are justified, we have peace with God.

Sanctification

In basic terms, sanctification means both to *be* holy, justified on the basis of the finished work of Christ, and to be *becoming* holy, less of a sinner and more a child of God. It refers to both a present holiness in community with God and also signifies an ongoing process of transformation in the Christian life.

In contrast to justification where we cannot be more or less justified, sanctification *is* a matter of more or less. Sanctification is to be lived, understood, and characterized by this truth. And what is holiness? If sanctification in living spirituality is about being and becoming holy, it is crucial to have the holy God in view.

God is Holy

When it comes to holiness we should begin with God, the Holy One. The scriptural map indicates that God is holy and calls his people to be holy. God is the great "I Am" (Ex.3:14) who speaks and acts from an infinite perspective. This God of Scripture is holy like no other and therefore sets the standard for holiness.

It is intriguing that in the ancient Near Eastern context the Israelites were called to be a holy people (Ex. 19:5-6). God the Holy One had brought them out of Egypt as both their redeemer and defender. His people were to be set apart. Godly holiness was in short supply in the neighboring polytheistic communities, and Israel was to reflect something of God's holiness in their own community, and to the other nations.

The people of Israel were intended to be different from other nations. They were the people of a holy God which came with certain responsibilities: being the light to the nations, having no idols, acting with equal weights and measures, and caring for the poor, the alien, the widows, and loving God (Lev. 19; Deut. 6). Why was this the case? God the Creator was their God, and being in community with this God meant being radically different in attitude, action, thought, and worship from all other nations. These

105

people were to be set apart so that all the earth would come to know that God was God.

Jesus Christ is Holy

We find a remarkable continuity of holiness in the person, mission and ministry of Jesus. He reflects what we have seen concerning God's holiness. Jesus was holy in both character and in meeting and fulfilling the requirements of the law. No one can be compared to him. Neither the emperor, nor the Jewish religious elite were holy. As the writer of Hebrews points out, Jesus is our great *forever* High Priest, the Holy Son, who was tempted as we are, yet was without sin.

And as Matthew's gospel records it in the Sermon on the Mount (5:48), Jesus stresses the need to be perfect as our heavenly Father is perfect. The Leviticus 19 imagery clearly demonstrates to Jesus' followers the importance of living holy lives.

The Spirit is Holy

After the resurrection and Jesus' earthly absence, the Holy Spirit arrives as a gift and the presence of the crucified and risen One himself. The Holy Spirit personally provides us with community with God. I believe that if the Holy Spirit had not come, Christianity would have slowly ground to a halt. There would have been no ongoing, vital connection between Jesus' followers and God. The arrival of the Holy Spirit establishes a holy continuity with what had come previously, thereby affirming the holiness of the Father and the Son. The Holy Spirit writes not on tablets of stone, but on hearts that follow Jesus Christ.

Being and Becoming Holy

It is essential to be aware that as Christians we are holy and becoming holy—sanctified in Christ Jesus. That is, we again find ourselves in the tension of already and not yet. We are in-between *being* holy on the basis of the finished work of Christ and our appropriation of this through faith, and *becoming* holy when we will be more fully and completely like Christ.

God has a marvelous promise for those who follow the path of the crucified and risen One. By God's grace, we are being transformed into the image of Christ. This reality and truth has extraordinary implications that are intimately connected to living spirituality. Our orientation and destination are not back to the creational garden, but to a past before time and to a future beyond it. I hope that this statement provokes you to reflect on this carefully.

Think for a moment about Adam and Eve and Christ. Adam and Eve imaged God, but Christ images God in a greater way than they ever could have. Adam and Eve were created. Christ is divine and pre-existent. And post-incarnation in his life, mission, death and resurrection, he became everlasting. He now lives forever, he who had no beginning, and who has no end.

Here we find the past before the garden and the future beyond it aligned. This perspective clearly explains why those who follow Christ are able to break out of and surpass the garden, and do not have it or its images as their destiny. Being transformed into the image of Christ is to image one who both precedes and goes beyond creation as we know it. This means that our imaging transformation has a present and everlasting significance. That is, Christians are now marked out as the living redeemed in that they follow the crucified and risen One, which means they are a testimony to the assured promise that the life they have is never-ending and not conditional.

Think carefully about this powerful reality, and then live it forever. Surely, we see here that the grace of God extends beyond all that we could ask or imagine. Superabundance.

Christians are being transformed. We are being and becoming like Christ, not Adam and Eve. This is our trajectory. We have Christ himself as our model, and it is Christ who we are to become like as we seek to practice the call to love God and all people.

Imaging Christ, for Christians, is the marvel of all marvels, the graciousness of all grace, and the love of all love.

Both/And: Sanctification in Degrees

Now that we have a grasp on holiness, let's return to its both/and *degree* character in living spirituality. Holiness is one of the core characteristics of living spirituality, and unfortunately we profoundly misunderstand it.

That misunderstanding of holiness starts with confusion. And that confusion may be due to the fact that much Christian teaching on spirituality these days is polarized. We are taught to view life in a manner that forces us to take opposing either/or positions which frequently harm, instead of helping our spirituality.

Take for example this typical configuration: either one is a child of God or a sinner. Many Christians would respond that this is the case. Yet neither of these poles is able to explain or contain the reality of the Christian life. The truth of the matter is that Christians are in tension as *both* God's children *and* sinners at the same time.

At this stage, I want you to start thinking in degrees. The concept of degrees in a sanctified Christian life means that there is no all or nothing, no either/or when it comes to sanctification. These polarizations are unwarranted as well as unnecessary. Christians are neither exclusively God's children, nor exclusively sinners. As hard as we try to live without the both/and or degrees, it is impossible. In fact, to attempt to do so will severely impoverish spirituality.

Amber's story
Amber struggled with polarizations. A tendency to polarize things had been evident in her life since her student days or perhaps even since childhood. She found herself continually fighting extremes: perfect marks or failure, legalism or freedom, control or neglect. These either/or extremes identified Amber's life. Sliding back and

forth between poles led her to frustration, which she eventually tried to deal with by indulging in a number of dubious activities.

Amber had a difficult time in life. This was due, at least partially, to her Christian family background. Her father, a fairly close-minded pastor and her mother, a dominant yet fragile person, never seemed to understand her. They unwittingly had little capacity to offer Amber a world of her own, thus always forcing her into theirs. Her father, through his perfectionism, and her mother, through her manipulating, created a world of guilt for Amber as she continually saw herself as failing to measure up to their standards.

As a result of spending her adolescent years seeking to please her parents, Amber developed a way of dealing with herself and her situational contexts that drove her further into an identity crisis. Who was she? Was it possible to have a different view of life and a different world than that which her parents had given her? Where did God fit into it all? How was she to take some responsibility for her own life?

When Amber left home for college, she began to think more seriously about God and truth. She eventually converted to Christ after attending a series of campus discussions held by Christians and through which the Spirit powerfully worked. And she began to taste the living water offered to her by Jesus Christ.

During this period of her life things went better for Amber, although not much really changed with respect to her polarizing tendencies and extremes. She achieved high marks in her studies, made good friends at school, and looked forward to graduating and finding a good job and success. While Amber had converted to Christ, her conversion had little significant impact on her directions in life.

After graduation, she spent a considerable amount of time and effort looking for the perfect job that would allow her to advance and excel. Caught up in the whirlwind of achievement and approval, Amber suppressed her questions and longings for something more authentic and meaningful.

When she found her dream job, she threw herself into it whole heartedly, but got lost along the way. After four years of somewhat excessive drinking, a stressful high-powered life, and several horribly broken relationships, Amber was devastated and her life was on the rocks.

Her job as a press secretary, which was emotionally taxing yet rewarding, contributed to Amber's alcohol problem. Her fear of rejection increased, and the anxiety of failure brought out her perfectionism. At the same time, any success she had gave her a false sense of measuring up. Both fear and celebration led to the same end: getting drunk.

Amber's stressful life and over-indulgence in drinking created severe problems for developing serious relationships, especially with men. Several flirtations ended rather quickly, while others faltered after a period of time. Amber continually repeated the error of falling in love with the wrong kinds of men who abused her and played on her weaknesses.

Many other people appreciated Amber's tenacity. She worked well with her boss and her colleagues, and everyone appreciated her get-it-done attitude. Amber, however, began to recognize that she needed more than human appreciation. Sensing her greater need for a deeper reality and facing the diminishing role of Christ in her life, she started to spend more time with a group of Christians at a local church. Unfortunately, much of the teaching she received in that context mirrored her parents' perspectives. She continued to be taught that the path to a more spiritual life was found in either/or configurations. In short, polarizations were assumed to be spiritual.

This teaching merely reinforced her constant, mantra-like polarizing. She began to repeat over and over to herself, *either* I am God's child and will get it all right, *or* I am a sinner and I will get it all wrong. First, she attempted to find resolution in one direction. Then, when that failed, she attempted to find it in the other. She saw and understood each pole as diametrically opposed to the other.

When Amber came to L'Abri she was a Christian, but she also had serious questions about God, truth, spirituality, and reality. She finally decided she could no longer suppress these questions. She was interested in finding sufficient answers and explanations, and clearly God had brought her to a new place. It was essential that she develop a robust theology, because that is the basis for living spirituality.

During her time at Swiss L'Abri, Amber eventually came to realize that this slide from pole to pole brought about repetition of the same failures. She really was *both* a child of God *and* yet a sinner. Eventually, she was able to acknowledge her inability to live a polarized identity that forced her into one without the other. She gradually discovered that she had been presented with and had embraced false options that were powerless to bring about lasting change and a transformed life.

This is a classic case of false-option identity syndrome. It was already present in Amber's life and was reinforced by the Christian circles she moved in. Amber is not alone. In many Christian contexts the aim of spirituality is to eliminate the both/and degree factor and any tension in regards to sanctification, but this type of polarization only leads to defeat in that it short circuits the transforming motion and power of God at work, and results in impoverished spirituality.

Amber is not solely a sinner, because she is also a child of God. She is washed, cleansed, justified in Christ, sanctified, and empowered by the Spirit. Neither is she solely a child of God, because she is also a sinner. She embraces and falls into sinful patterns of gossip, and being selfish and unloving. For the present, the composite of these is her identity. The reality of sin is evident in her life, but so is the reality of grace in that she is God's child.

We can configure it this way. We start with the affirmation that Amber is a Christian. When she believes, she is *justified* before God on the basis of the finished work of Christ. As we have seen, there are no degrees when it comes to being a Christian. One is either a Christian or not a Christian.

The second affirmation is that Amber is *both* sanctified *and* becoming sanctified in degrees, demonstrating that growth and change are possible. Amber is actually changing and becoming more like Christ after she believed. Her gradual transformation bears testimony to the reality that the Spirit is continually at work in her life.

Let me state it this way. We are on the way to becoming fully sanctified—imaging Christ through the power of the Spirit. As we move in this direction, we will find ourselves attaining different degrees of this ultimate destiny. When it comes to sanctification, some of us will be living sanctified lives in lesser degrees, while others are living sanctified lives in greater degrees, and this may fluctuate in different areas. Yet, no one is ever completely sanctified in this life. That awaits a future reality. There's always room to move ahead toward the goal of more faithfully imaging Christ.

At this point, it is important to recall that being holy corresponds on the one hand to God's declaration that those who are justified in Christ are his beloved children. On the other hand, becoming holy allows room for degrees and recognizes that Christians continue to sin and therefore are not yet fully who they in some sense already are.

When one is a Christian, sin does not overthrow justification. We sin, but this does not stop us from *being holy*, because the holiness is based on the finished work of Christ (justified/sanctified). Neither do we stop *becoming holy* (moving to full sanctification in the power of the Spirit) on the basis of this same finished work. No doubt, we lose the path, but through the map and the action of the Holy Spirit rediscovery is always a present possibility. Sin is horrid, destructive, and requires repentance, but it is incapable of thoroughly devastating a child of God.

Romans 6 comes back to mind here. The perpetual cycle of sin can diminish and eventually be done away with. After all, this is what sanctification means. It is a dynamic movement of *being and becoming* holy in greater and greater degrees.

Being a Zero

We can also look at this dynamic movement of a both/and sanctification in degrees from another angle that will help us reverse spiritual impoverishment. Some Christians claim to be living a radical life for God, and in principle I have no problem with this. Yet the way that it is put forward today can be unhelpful and fairly misleading.

Such a claim, at least as it has been frequently stated to me, means that we are truly spiritual when we seek to diminish ourselves and become zeroes. The radical life then is often described as *total* abandonment to God. This translates into, God does not want us to use our minds, hearts, imaginations, and wills, but instead to close everything down, withdraw, and let go. *Get out of the way* and *take no responsibilities* are assumed to be truly and ultimately spiritual. It goes something like this: the more we attempt to be zeroes, the more spiritual we are; we either adopt being zeroes or we're not spiritual.

Denial and rejection of ourselves, it is often said, will illuminate the path toward Christian spirituality. The aim is to banish tension and find harmony with God. Tension is unspiritual and resolution is spiritual. Sanctification is getting rid of ourselves. If we can only accomplish this, we will supposedly attain a spiritual life with God. To put it mildly, this is an impoverished notion of Christian spirituality, which disregards sanctification and ignores a both/and of tensional degrees, rather than embracing them.

From a biblical perspective, when it comes to sanctification, this either/or type of polarization is dubious, yet many Christians fall prey to the assumption that it is a more holy or spiritual direction for the Christian life. No doubt, this point of view sounds extremely attractive, even spiritual, but it fails to cohere to or with the map of Scripture.

The major problem with this either/or view of sanctification (either a zero or not spiritual) is its presentation of an idealism that, in the end, leads us to an unspiritual resolution. The tyranny of false options, as expressed in an either/or configuration, is devastating. Sanctification is simply not like that.

In spite of brokenness, God redeems and sanctifies us. He wants us to use our minds, hearts, imaginations, and wills in a creative and sanctified manner that sufficiently affirms and demonstrates that God is there, that we are God's children, and that this is God's world.

Think for a moment about the creational mandate (Genesis 1 and 9) for God's images to be fruitful and multiply; humans are to be stewards of the earth—to care for it as God does. Images are to carry out a task. How could a zero have a task?

Furthermore, Jesus taught his disciples to be salt and light (Matthew 5:13-16). Being salt and light speaks of personal and cultural assessment and engagement, not withdrawal. How could the disciples accomplish this if they were supposed to be zeroes in order to be spiritual?

Later, Paul exhorted Christians not to be conformed to this age, but to be transformed by the renewing of the mind (Romans 12:2), so that they might be able to discern the will of God. How could Christians do this by becoming nobodies?

To be stewards of the earth, to be salt and light, and to be transformed by the renewing of the mind show that God configures us into a position of accountability. Take responsibility *and* depend on God. Affirm the indwelling of the Holy Spirit *and* use your abilities to serve God and others. Clearly, living spirituality sanctification is about much more than this, but certainly not about any less.

Sanctification is not being and becoming zero selves, but being and becoming new selves, creationally and salvifically, in Christ. Sanctification is about being and becoming a true self, not a nobody. God affirms our sanctified actions and is pleased with them as they increase and have an impact on the world as a demonstration of living spirituality, and for the sake of Christ.

Christians are those in community with God; we are sanctified, and we are in the process of becoming fully sanctified. We have received the gift of the Spirit, and the power of the resurrection is at work in our lives, as Ephesians 1 so plainly states. All of this is far from being and becoming a zero or indulging in the practice of self-effacement.

In my view, the false-option, either/or perspective is not the way toward illuminating the path of living spirituality. On the contrary, it results in a paralyzing polarization. This outlook assumes a static state of sanctification for Christian spirituality— once a zero always a zero. There is no sanctifying *motion* toward God, there is no relation *and* distinction between God and us, and there is no *tension* of being a child of God and a sinner. When all this is added up, sanctification is not living, but dormant.

Thankfully, the map of Scripture shows that this is not our path. Though we are sinners, we have the gift of living that grace-filled promise of being continually transformed into the image of Christ.

Position and Condition

Another useful way of viewing the both/and degree perspective of sanctification is the configuration of a *position-condition* dynamic for disciples of Jesus.

Here's what I mean. We have already seen Romans 6 clearly affirm that when we identify with and are integrated into Christ's death and resurrection, we have a new orientation. This means that we have received a *position* before God based on his grace.

When we accept the finished work of Christ, we are released from the orientation of sin and death, reckoned righteous, and oriented to life in community with God. That is, through this reckoning by God, Christians are declared to be holy: justified/sanctified. My term for this is receiving God's gift of a *position*.

In addition to this, Christians still have a *condition*, which is not yet their *position*. How does this work out? From a biblical perspective, I believe that Christians are *both* holy *and* becoming holy. As we have seen, we are *both* children of God *and* sinners.

We find a prime example of this in Paul's letter to the Corinthians. In 1 Corinthians 1:2 the apostle refers to the Christians at Corinth as those sanctified: those *holy* in Christ and those called to be *holy*. He then goes on in his letter to critique them for, among other things, their immaturity and divisions. The apostle chastises them on a number of accounts for an alarming degree of incongruity between their *position* (holy) and *condition* (the need to become holy). This incongruity is evident when you read the rest of the letter, especially in chapters 3-4, but Paul never retracts the affirmation that they are holy, because they have believed in Christ and are therefore justified.

Hebrews also addresses this profound truth. In 10:1-14, we read two statements in particular that apply to our discussion of sanctification. First, that Christians *have been made* holy through the sacrifice of the body of Jesus Christ, once and for all (verse 10). Second, notice that through this same sacrifice that has made them perfect forever, they are also *being made* holy (verse 14).

The writer of Hebrews captures the tensional perspective of a both/and perspective. We are *both* children of God *and* sinners. In living spirituality however, our position as a gift of grace begins to overarch our condition as we become more holy through our being in community with God. This happens because we are being transformed, and to a greater extent imaging Christ. At some point in the future, when redemption is complete, our condition will be entirely traced over, and our position will become the whole of who we are as we move further into everlasting life with God. This trajectory leaves us in a dynamic tension that characterizes living spirituality. But what a tension—being holy and becoming holy—living in community with God.

Prescriptive and Preventative

We are now going to look at a final example of how polarization negatively affects sanctification and results in impoverished spirituality. In reversing this polarization, we will again see the value of a theologically appropriate both/and orientation.

I want to explore the terms *prescriptive* and *preventative*. These terms may be familiar in a medical context—and indeed they relate to the spiritual health of Christians. I will use them here to highlight an important double-edged truth for living spirituality, but first let's focus on the blood of Christ from a theological angle.

Shedding animal blood was a pivotal part of sacrifice under the old covenant priesthood and it provisionally opened the way for God to have community with his people. But the blood of bulls and goats was never able to entirely deal with sin. There was a need for a greater sacrifice, and this need was met by the blood of Christ.

As our great high priest, Christ enters once and for all into the most holy place: the place where God dwells. There is no repetition necessary. The blood of the pre-existent, crucified and risen One, secures everlasting redemption. He washes us—not with animal blood which can never purify and cleanse—but with his own divine blood.

Christ sheds his blood on our behalf so that we too might enter into community with God and be wholly cleansed. He does so with a blood of divine quality that, in its shedding, has divine consequences for our lives. Without blood—the blood of Christ—the covenant is not fulfilled, we are not released from sin, we are not justified, and there is no sanctification.

117

Now that we have the theological perspective in place, I want to explain how the *prescriptive* view works. I suggest that Christian spirituality today tends to focus on the more *prescriptive* dimension of the blood of Christ. Christians would agree that Christ has died for our sins and that his shed blood is essential for redemption, yet impoverishment surfaces in envisioning this in a one dimensional manner. That is, we treat the blood of Christ solely as a *prescription* from God.

We go to God when we sin and he gives us a prescription for the blood of Christ. This prescription will make us well, both now and again the next time we sin. Numerous maladies and sicknesses take us to a doctor to get a prescription. When we take the medicine prescribed we usually improve and are restored to health. If we apply this imagery to the way God works, we can say that it is through the prescription of the blood of Christ that we are made well after sinning. We can go back to God again and again when we sin and God will give us the prescription. The blood of Christ is the remedy, and when we confess our sin, God is faithful to release us and we start anew.

There is no question that this is indeed true, and we should be thankful for the offer and capacity of divine blood shed on our behalf to heal us. The blood of Christ cleanses, renews, and thus provides a way for us to enter and re-enter into living community with God, and to be in real community with each other. And this is crucial to living spirituality, but there is more to it than the prescription view suggests.

Impoverishment enters, for many Christians, when the efficacy of the blood of Christ is seen to only function in this way. Two particular problems arise. First, this is an inadequate view of sanctification and spirituality. Second, it is a deficient perspective of the blood of Christ. These two problems can best be illustrated by the following story.

Don's story

Don worked with fellow Christians at a mission. The mission had a long history of assisting many people, although over the years it encountered struggles and complications. There was some in-fighting and a growing lack of trust among the staff.

One of Don's colleagues grew vindictive and began to treat him with suspicion. Don wondered what was going on. He began to notice repeated jabs that made relating to this person difficult. After each wounding comment, Don's colleague would be very apologetic. He would come to Don and ask for his forgiveness. This scenario continued to go on for sometime, and it posed significant questions for Don. How did such an attitude, and the comments that went with it, fit in with a Christian view of sanctification and spirituality?

At this stage, Don tried to envision what his colleague's request for forgiveness really amounted to. Was the apology sincere? What did forgiveness mean for this person? Would the pattern of betrayal really change? After another incident and apology, Don was optimistic that everything had been cleared up; however, two weeks later his colleague repeated the same thing again.

Don began to understand. He realized that his colleague viewed each apology as a release from an isolated sinful action that had no effect on subsequent behavior. This person thought that the sanctified Christian life was *entirely* about the cycle of sin and forgiveness. In other words, it was solely *prescriptive*.

Don eventually came to the conclusion that such an impoverished spirituality stemmed from an inadequate notion of sanctification, which in the case of his colleague was static and prescriptive. That is, sanctification carried with it no responsibility to work towards change to prevent further sin the next time around. God provided the prescription of the blood of Christ. He took it, and that was the end of the matter. Sadly, this type of situation is widespread in many Christian circles.

119

Thankfully, Don came to understand that the blood of Christ has a more dynamic role than that. It is not only prescriptive, but also *preventative*. And here's where impoverishment can diminish. While the blood of Christ renews and cleanses a follower of the crucified and risen One, it also should have a *preventative* dimension that helps us change our sinful patterns as we face similar circumstances. There may not always be change, but we should be seeking transformation with regard to our sin. If we remain in the same cycle of sin, our sanctification is dormant, and the blood of Christ has little or no *preventative* role in our lives.

A prescriptive view of the blood of Christ is essential, but all too frequently it merely affirms the status quo: sin. Don's colleague never changed, at least as far as Don knew, but that's to be lamentably expected in holding to such a limited view of the role of the blood of Christ.

The addition of a preventative dynamic here does not mean that we can be entirely without sin. There will always be an abundance of sin in our lives to keep this from being the case. Sanctification, however, is about release from present sin and changing sinful practices in light of this. What happens is that some areas of sin in our lives will get better and stay better, and we will actually stop committing those particular sins.

The blood of Christ is both prescriptive and preventative, which, in conjunction with the power of the Spirit in our lives, can bring about change from the deadly cycles of sin. Sanctification is comprised of this both/and of the blood of Christ, and such a view is directly connected to living spirituality.

12

Knowledge

The journey continues. Now we are going to look at how the important issue of knowledge is to be configured in living spirituality. Knowledge and spirituality are closely connected in our lives and if we are to be living spirituality, we need to reverse the spiritual impoverishment connected to some of the questionable views of knowledge that are prominent today.

Many people come to L'Abri searching, and we give them honest answers to honest questions. Some of these people are demanding to know if Christianity is true. What these types of seekers are often really expecting is to be able to know that Christianity is true in the same way that God would know something is true. They want to know with a total one hundred percent certainty.

My response to this expectation has been that we cannot know (anything) in such a way, and that in fact to demand one hundred percent knowledge is a violation of the Creator/creature relationship and therefore a sin. If we demand the same degree of knowledge that God has, we falsify our creaturely status, and in so doing move into a cycle of sinful and dying spirituality.

However, I also strongly stress that it would be an equally sinful violation of this Creator/creature relationship to say that we do not have any knowledge of God or of anything else. We do have credible knowledge of many things, and God claims to have revealed himself *sufficiently* in creation, history, the scriptural map, the Spirit, word and action, for us have sufficient knowledge that he is there and that Christianity is true. If we want to say that this revelation is either *total* or that it is *non-existent*, we are stepping outside our bounds as creatures and putting ourselves in God's place and this inevitably leads to impoverishment.

The Dangers of Being Overly Vague or Certain

Christians are facing two dangers: becoming as entirely ambiguous, or as exhaustively certain as anyone else on matters of knowledge. When it comes to knowledge, we too often tend to embrace the perspective of *total* ambiguity or *complete* certainty, in exchange for sufficient knowledge, which is truly spiritual. In what direction should we move to foster living spirituality?

We have already discussed the relevance of several theological perspectives in order to clarify the meaning of living spirituality. Without leaving these perspectives behind, let's explore how a Christian view of knowledge might help us to counter totalizing notions and influences that impoverish spirituality. There are a matrix of problems concerning knowledge and the Christian faith, but I want to focus on two powerful options that are often presented as our *only* options.

These options represent two worldviews and pictures of knowledge. The first expresses a relativist mentality and rests on the notion that everything is equally ambiguous. All that's clear is that nothing is clear. This signifies *total* ambiguity, although those who hold this view would be adamant that this was not the case, because anything total is thought to go against the very DNA of relativism.

The second option is based on the argument that everything is totally clear, and if we all would just think about it rationally, we would see the truth in the same way. This stands for *total* clarity and characterizes those who are always right, because they think they have exhaustive knowledge.

Should Christians adopt or accept either of these portrayals of knowledge and worldview as legitimate expressions of living spirituality? Wisdom suggests otherwise. These types of options evoke an unsustainable and unlivable contradiction: a false absolutizing.

After all, as finite human beings we can only live on the basis of what we know. Our knowledge is limited yet sufficient, and therefore does not correspond to either option. If this is the case, neither worldview can claim totality. Finite human beings always know something, not nothing or everything. I have often been told that it is those who claim to know nothing that are humble and that it is those who claim to know everything that are arrogant. My view is that both, in the end, are positions of pride since neither is true according to the scriptural map.

Such false views or options concerning knowledge are disconnected from the truth. When we assume that everything is up for grabs and that nothing is clear, or that we have comprehensive knowledge and all is certain, we have chosen to go against the mapping of Scripture, reality, and all that it means to be human in God's world.

Balancing Accounts, People, and Knowledge

Living spirituality acknowledges the importance of recognizing that the knower is always involved in the knowing. This does not mean, however, that knowledge is merely a subjective enterprise that allows us to believe whatever we would like. Still, we are always involved in knowing what we do know. Let's consider a few examples to make the point.

Think about your bank account. Not the contents or lack thereof, but in reference to the truth that knowledge is not just what we make up as we go along. You may assume that you know your bank balance only to have that knowledge modified. You may know that you have a certain amount of money in the bank, but unless the bank affirms this knowledge, you may be mistaken. And the bank will certainly inform you when you overdraw or bounce a check on the basis of what you thought you knew. This is not to say that banks never make mistakes. The point I'm after is to show that our knowledge claims are dependent on and reinforced by external criteria that we are involved in, but that we are not the source or origin of creating.

A second example is other people. You and I do not create them. They are there and make themselves known to us in an objective manner. They are not there because we subjectively make them be. We quickly find this out through a difference of opinion or an attempt to occupy the same physical space. Our knowledge of the existence of other people is related to our subjectivity, but it is not merely a product of it. Other people radically impact who we are. They change us and contribute to our lives.

In order to clarify, the knower is always involved in the knowing, yet this truth does not necessitate that we have no true knowledge. Let me remind you here of the *degree* perspective that was developed in the last chapter. As we seek to know more about God, truth and the whole of life, there will always be a degree of knowledge and of ambiguity, and this degree mode is far from the dogmatic assertions of totalities. Neither total ambiguity nor total knowledge are real or viable options, because both are utopist and escape us all—they leave us far from the truth and the scriptural map. Being humans in God's created world forces us into a different view. That is, finite life is lived in degrees, not totalities.

Through the Mirror Dimly

As I have previously pointed out and the map of Scripture affirms, we who are in community with God through Jesus Christ and living in the power of the Spirit are already *living* spirituality. And how does this apply to knowledge? Does this mean that ambiguity is entirely absent? This is highly unlikely. The map itself leaves a number of things open, although it also brings closure to a variety of others.

What we want to embrace is the *sufficiency* of knowledge where anyone is free to evaluate, test, and interact with Christian truth claims. The Christian connection between knowledge and spirituality is expressed through a confession and an affirmation: Christians do not have exhaustive knowledge, but we do have sufficient knowledge.

When Christians take the role of "know-it-alls" or "know-nothings," they are contributing to impoverished spirituality. A living spirituality reversal of this impoverishment should evoke a life of tension between *confidence* and *humility*. We have good and sufficient reasons and can confidently know that Christianity is true, but there is also a place for humility in recognition that we don't have all the information necessary for a neutrally perceived knowledge that is exhaustive. An over-emphasis in one direction or the other detracts from community with God, the centrality of Christ, the work of the Spirit, and Christian identity in the world.

The apostle Paul is making a similar point in his letter to Corinth, which I summarize as, "Now, we see through a glass darkly or in a mirror dimly, but when Christ returns we will see face to face" (1 Cor. 13:12). A careful study of this chapter reminds us that we still await the day when Christ returns. This powerful truth is to be taken seriously into account when it comes to our views of knowledge, as we live spirituality in the present.

On the day of Christ's return, the redeeming activity of God in the world and in his children will be complete. As we wait for the arrival of the *day* of Christ, there is already a present redemption that helps us—in spite of our sinfulness—to see more clearly, although this clarity never gives us perfect vision or exhaustive knowledge.

This scenario reminds us of our tensional perspective concerning the whole of living spirituality. Notice that we again have an *already* and *not yet* dynamic when it comes to the question of knowledge. As Christians we *already* have sufficient knowledge about God, the work of creation and salvation, and a host of other things, but we do *not yet* have the fullness of knowledge that will only come when we see God face to face.

13

Facing Adversity

Facing adversity is a significant challenge for living spirituality. This key issue cannot be ignored or avoided, as adversity is going to be part of the Christian life. How are we to handle adversity when it comes our way? What kinds of responses are appropriate in adverse situations? In this chapter we are going to delve into Paul's letter to the Philippians, one of our most insightful markers on the map for living spirituality, especially when things don't go as we hope and the path gets rough.

Whether living centuries ago in Philippi or today in the current millennium, Christians facing adversity would benefit from a closer reading of this remarkable letter. We are going to focus on several of its key sections that will direct us to living spirituality.

The Philippians were struggling to find their way. They encountered external opposition and grappled with internal problems. These two forces in their lives, combined with a deep concern for the fate of the apostle Paul, had begun to defeat them. Their hope for a present and future living spirituality was diminishing, and this began to put their *joy* in Christ in peril. As a result of their own struggles, and those of their dear friend, Paul, they needed wisdom, counsel, and direction to move them ahead on the journey.

We repeatedly find ourselves in similar circumstances. Difficult and sometimes complex situations can confront us on the path of life. At times, we too are at risk of losing our joy in Christ. Our journey is laborious and riddled with precarious moments that can stretch into hours, days, months, even years. When personal or family clashes threaten us, worry for a loved one haunts us, or disagreements with others in our community of faith creates questions and conflict, we need trust, healthy suspicion, and wise guidance. In short, we have much in common with our Philippian predecessors.

The letter to the Philippians is often referred to as a "friendly" letter. That is, there was a close relationship between these believers and the apostle Paul. Compared to other letters Paul wrote, this one contains little doctrinal confrontation and minimal apologetics.

The apostle seeks to encourage and exhort believers to press on in their faith, to recognize who they are in Christ, and to embrace *joy* in the midst of their present adverse circumstances. His letter offers counsel and direction for living spiritually in the present situations of our lives. Paul's wisdom will benefit us as we look more deeply at several sections of his letter.

Philippians 1:1-11: Greeting, Thanksgiving and Prayer

(1) Paul and Timothy, servants of Christ Jesus, to all the saints in Christ Jesus at Philippi, together with the overseers and deacons: (2) Grace and peace to you from God our Father and the Lord Jesus Christ. (3) I thank my God every time I remember you. (4) In all my prayers for all of you, I always pray with joy (5) because of your partnership in the gospel from the first day until now, (6) being confident of this, that he who began a good work in you will carry it on to completion until the day of Christ Jesus. (7) It is right for me to feel this way about all of you, since I have you in my

heart; for whether I am in chains or defending and confirming the gospel, all of you share in God's grace with me. (8) God can testify how I long for all of you with the affection of Christ Jesus. (9) And this is my prayer; that your love may abound more and more in knowledge and depth of insight, (10) so that you may be able to discern what is best and may be pure and blameless until the day of Christ, (11) filled with the fruit of righteousness that comes through Jesus Christ—to the glory and praise of God.

One of the most important elements of good map reading is to understand the dynamics of context. My aim here is to establish the literary and theological context for the passages that we are going to look at more closely in chapter two.

The greeting, thanksgiving and prayer hint at some of the issues that Paul will address throughout the letter. He writes of God beginning a good work which will be brought to completion on the day of Christ (1:6; 4:19).

The apostle asks God that the Philippians' *love* may grow in knowledge and depth of insight, *so that* they might be able to discern what is best and be blameless until the day of Christ. In short, that *love* may be a product of wisdom, *so that* they may live it wisely. What a magnificent request. Paul knows well that the Christian life is not a simple list of rights and wrongs. To grow in love we need knowledge, insight and discernment.

How often do we mirror this type of prayer for ourselves and others? If you are like me, perhaps not often enough. We are to view discernment and blamelessness as being deeply connected to growing in love. To grow in love and to discern should lead us in the direction of being blameless. Facing adversity requires wise love in order for Christians to live spirituality in the shadow of the coming day of Christ.

We can already see that the "day of Christ" is important to this letter and to living spirituality. And the apostle will return to it again in chapters two and three. His affirmation here is that something of God's sanctifying work has *already* begun in the Philippians' lives, but he also wants Christians to be aware that there is a day coming at some point in the future when Christ will reign not only over their lives, but over everything.

Philippians 1:12-26: What Purpose?

(12) Now I want you to know, brothers, that what has happened to me has really served to advance the gospel. (13) As a result, it has become clear throughout the whole palace guard and to everyone else that I am in chains for Christ. (14) Because of my chains, most of the brothers in the Lord have been encouraged to speak the word of God more courageously and fearlessly.

(15) It is true that some preach Christ out of envy and rivalry, but others out of goodwill. (16) The latter do so in love, knowing that I am put here for the defense of the gospel. (17) The former preach Christ out of selfish ambition, not sincerely, supposing that they can stir up trouble for me while I am in chains. (18) But what does it matter? The important thing is that in every way, whether from false motives or true, Christ is preached. And because of this I rejoice.

Yes, and I will continue to rejoice, (19) for I know that through your prayers and the help given by the Spirit of Jesus Christ, what has happened to me will turn out for my deliverance (20) I eagerly expect and hope that I will in no way be ashamed, but will have sufficient courage so that now as always Christ will be exalted in my body, whether by life or by death. (21) For to me, to live is Christ and to die is gain. (22) If I am to go on living in the body, this will mean fruitful labor for me. Yes what shall I choose? I do not know! (23) I am torn between the two: I desire to depart and be with Christ, which is better by far; (24) but it is more necessary for you that I remain in the body. (25) Convinced of this, I know that I will remain, and I will continue with all of you for your progress

*and joy in the faith, (26) so that through my being with you again
your joy in Christ will overflow on account of me.*

In this section, Paul writes of his present adverse circumstances.
What should he do at this point? What is his purpose? He likely
wants his readers to know what is happening in his life. At the same
time, he wants to encourage them by his example in regard to their
own present situation. For Paul, adversity does not equate
hopelessness. And the magnitude of this is essential for us to grasp.

For example, the apostle's imprisonment has turned out for
good in that the gospel has gone forward in spite of adversity.
Though Paul had faced life-threatening circumstances, his ability to
rejoice in Christ remained intact. The tremendously significant
lesson to learn here is this: Paul's spirituality was not focused on
his present adversity, but rather on how to view his present situation
from a larger, Christ-focused context.

Living spirituality is far larger than what we can see from our
adverse circumstances. It is rooted in the gospel of the incarnation,
life, death, resurrection, and second coming of the crucified and
risen One. While our adversity is important and not to be minimized
or ignored, it is crucial that we realize we are looking at it through a
horizon that actually transcends and goes beyond it.

We are often in danger of becoming so present-focused on our
adversity that we can only see the "x" on the path that tells us "you
are here." To illuminate the path for living spirituality, we need to
view our present location on the path as part of a broader pathway,
which includes the scriptural mapping of our journey. We are not to
view our present adversity as the referent for itself. *Reflect intensely
on this.*

Those who follow Christ are not to regard this broader mapping
of living spirituality as an escape from adversity. Far from it. The
map points us toward shaping a new present from which to
understand our place on the path. Another way of picturing this is to

think of it as taking a *long view* of our lives in reference to the destination of the path on the map.

Such a long view is ultimately focused on the day of Christ, the day when the risen, glorified Christ returns and we will see God face to face. When we take that view, we are setting the context for our *short view*: our present difficulty. In embracing this long view, we gain an important perspective on how to view the gravity of our present adverse circumstances and situations.

What's taking place here is the battle of *presents*. One present context on the short view is rife with deathly difficulties: fear of others, conflicts, oppression, opposition, anxiety. The other present context is a long view filled with life and community with God and his people, as we live in and look forward to the day of Christ. This battle of *presents* corresponds to a tensional perspective inside us where the first present is marked by its temporal character and the second by that which is everlasting.

However, it is imperative to remember Paul's assurance to the Philippians: adversity is relatively short term and therefore does not have the power to destroy our joy in Christ, which is a *forever* joy. This joy is neither a joy of adversity, nor a joy of naiveté, but a joy *in spite* of our adversity. It is a joy of knowing that *because of* our day-of-Christ destination, we have a present perspective that enables us to endure in the midst of adverse circumstances. This won't make them go away, but it does release us from the despair of hopelessness.

Philippians 1:27-30: Stand Firm

(27) Whatever happens, conduct yourselves in a manner worthy of the gospel of Christ. Then, whether I come and see you or only hear about you in my absence, I will know that you stand firm in one sprit, contending as one man for the faith of the gospel (28) without being frightened in any way by those who oppose you. This is a sign to them that they will be destroyed, but that you will be saved—and

that by God. (29) For it has been granted to you on behalf of Christ not only to believe on him, but also to suffer for him, (30) since you are going through the same struggle you saw I had, and now hear that I still have.

Now we turn to the last section of the first chapter. Paul exhorts Christians to stand firm for the faith of the gospel irrespective of their present problems. We are not to fear external opposition, because God will save us.

Notice this does not mean that we may not *suffer* for Christ's sake. That is a constant reality that we all face, yet we are not to allow it to overwhelm us to the point of despondency. Such adversity and conflict are not to totally determine our present spirituality.

External opposition: Connie's story

Connie found it harder and harder to be a follower of Christ. She received little support at home or at college. Being a Christian seemed to have few advantages and many drawbacks, as Connie was excluded from college parties or other social events that her classmates attended. Her colleagues at her part-time job ridiculed her because she was a Christian and made fun of her moral standards. She was facing adversity and not quite sure how to handle it.

Fortunately, Connie became involved in a Christian community and found encouragement through the help and support of others. The opposition she faced at home, college and work was severe and almost overwhelming; however, by focusing on the reality of the *long view* she was able to stand firm for the gospel.

Connie began to discover that there was more from which to live her spirituality than the present adversity she faced. Although she was facing external opposition that caused her suffering, this did not need to defeat her or rob her of her joy in Christ. Solidarity with others of like mind, heart and spirit gave her sustenance. This enabled her to be more confident that, in spite of adversity, she could take the long view and follow the path to life.

What can we learn from Philippians and Connie? When we face external opposition, we must seek the support of Christians that we trust—kindred spirits—with whom we can find encouragement and experience unity. In adverse circumstances remember the *long view*. A focus on the day of Christ and our destiny will enable us to have joyful community in Christ, in spite of present difficulties.

Philippians 2:1-4: "If's" and Disintegration

(1) If you have any encouragement from being united with Christ, if any comfort from his love, if any fellowship with the Spirit, if any tenderness and compassion, (2) then make my joy complete by being like-minded, having the same love, being one in spirit and purpose.(3) Do nothing out of selfish ambition or vain conceit, but in humility consider others better than yourselves. (4) Each of you should look not only to your own interests, but also to the interests of others.

In the first chapter, Paul has already called believers to live their lives in a manner worthy of the gospel of Christ as they face *external* opposition. He now moves on to address the danger of *internal* disintegration in chapter two. The apostle begins with a passionate plea that we desperately need to hear today if we hope to contribute to a reversal of spiritual impoverishment. This is not dogmatic theology, but an extraordinary appeal for unity and a concern for the other.

Verse 1 gives us four *if* clauses that should be understood as "since" or "as is the case." These first four clauses speak of realities that have *already* taken place in believers' lives to some degree.

Paul writes, "*If* there is any comfort in Christ, *if* any encouragement from his love, *if* any participation or fellowship in the Spirit, *if* any tender mercy and compassion."

The apostle is seeking to persuade believers on the basis of these present realities that they must be careful to avoid internal disintegration. This four-fold plea rests on what God has already been doing in the lives of these Christians, and Paul affirms that since this is the case concerning Christ, the Spirit, and God's activity, Christians should be unified.

Verse 2 then, on the basis of the truths of verse 1, makes a strong and loving appeal for unity. For Paul, the threat of disunity can result in diminished joy in Christ, and a loss of living spirituality. He exhorts Christians to have one mind: a unity of both thought and will. He urges them to have the same love—the love of Christ for each other. And he desires them to be one in Spirit and purpose—moving towards the same destination of living spirituality in community with God and each other. Paul clearly sees that division and strife will undermine unity and stifle the capacity for our love to grow in wisdom and depth of insight.

Let's look at a story that illustrates the danger of internal disintegration and highlights several responses that will hopefully move us in the direction of promoting unity in the midst of conflict.

Internal disintegration: Sarah's story

Sarah had known Heather for a couple of years. They had been through many challenges together and were good friends. They both were Christians and took their faith seriously. They shared similar tastes in music, art, film, and were well aware of the importance of ideas and their power to influence people. These common interests had enhanced their ongoing friendship and contributed to their views of living the Christian life.

For unknown reasons, at least to Sarah, the friendship began to deteriorate. Seemingly out of the blue, their discussions and interactions became tense. Sarah's perception of her friendship with Heather wavered. Every time Sarah talked with Heather, she sensed an edge from her friend that had not existed previously. Already frustrated and bewildered, Sarah grew anxious and insecure.

135

What would you do? How would you deal with this threat of *internal* disintegration? What do you do or have you done when fear, doubt, and suspicion make it difficult to maintain contact with those close to you?

Put yourself in this situation. You are Sarah. You visit your friend Heather for coffee and walk into her kitchen. Heather looks at you as if you just arrived from another planet. Her body gestures, lack of eye contact, and obvious discomfort say clearer than words: *What are you doing here? Go away.* You are left standing there wondering what happened.

Something, somewhere, has gone terribly wrong. You try to bring things out into the open, but nothing surfaces. After a painful bit of small talk, things grow more and more uncomfortable, and you decide to leave.

What is your attitude as you leave her house? Are you hurt and feeling rejected? I think it's safe to assume that most of us would feel this way. Rejection goes deep, and the hurt hollows our insides. Then inner strife grows—devastating, convoluting, and disorienting.

What is the way ahead? Usually, our tendency here is to either want to figure out a way to get back at Heather, or to avoid all contact that might expose us to more of the same. Our feelings all too often reign in these circumstances, and revenge or avoidance of adversity appear to be our only option.

Neither of these alternatives, however, is following the mapped-out path of unity in Christ. One of the chief characteristics of this unity is to be aware that as disciples of Jesus we are together on the path to life. It is essential to humbly invite the other person to share a vision for the direction ahead together. And sometimes this is an ongoing process.

To follow Christ means loving Heather in spite of her treatment of you. How audacious! This is not the way it's supposed to work. We are to shield ourselves at all costs. We are to treat others the way they treat us. *If* Heather treats me appropriately *then* I will respond in like manner: a conditional relationship.

But unity in Christ is not to be reduced to such self-centered protectionism or merely how you feel. Reversal of spiritual impoverishment is found elsewhere. That is, your relationship with the Heathers in your life is not based on how they treat or relate to you, but on Christ and how he relates to you both. From your side you have a responsibility to act as a follower of Christ, irrespective of immediate results. There are key questions to ask yourself: What is your view of sin? Where is Christ in your life? Who are you as God's child?

These may be painful questions to pose in the midst of internal conflict among Christians, but they are essential to living spirituality. Even though Heather decided to end the relationship, Sarah should still attempt to recover unity.

Practically this means that you return to her kitchen and work at moving the relationship towards restoration. This may take some time and even be arduous, but it is attempting to put the reality of the cross of Christ and the redemptive power of God to work in a broken situation. Brokenness is one of the places where being a Christian can and should make a difference. It is important to add that we are not to be naive. Things may never get better. We may have to take another course of mediation, but this should be the last resort, not the first.

In the face of internal disintegration, actions of grace, releasing, loving, and putting the other first are all part of our calling. We must seek to practically live out the love of Christ in unity, not just talk about it. Whether in the most basic or the most difficult circumstances, our model is the crucified and risen One.

Returning now to Paul's letter, we see the apostle brings this section to a close in verses 3-4 adding two, "Do not do this, but that" clauses. Selfish ambition, vanity, and conceit will all lead to division and unspiritual lives. In sharp contrast, *humility*, in considering others better than ourselves, will promote unity and

137

living spirituality. Though appropriate self interest is a virtue in Christ (see especially vs. 4), we are to constantly be aware of others and their interests.

Philippians 2:5-11: The Attitude of Christ

(5) Your attitude should be the same as that of Christ Jesus:

(6) Who, being in very nature God, did not consider equality with God something to be grasped,

(7) but made himself nothing, taking the very nature of a servant, being made in human likeness.

(8) And being found in appearance as a man, he humbled himself and became obedient to death— even death on a cross!

(9) Therefore God exalted him to the highest place and gave him the name that is above every name,

(10) that at the name of Jesus every knee should bow, in heaven and on earth and under the earth,

(11) and every tongue confess that Jesus Christ is Lord, to the glory of God the Father.

As we approach this key paragraph it is essential to recall the context of 2:1-4. Keep this in mind. Verses 5-11 also address the question of unity and humility, in addition to looking out for others interests. The paragraph is placed where it is in the letter for the express purpose of showing Christians what Christ's attitude was, and what their attitude should be.

It is helpful to see verses 6-8 and verses 9-11 as forming two parts. The first part focuses on Jesus' self-humbling, and the second describes his exaltation by the Father. This division captures the dynamic movement in Jesus' life and allows us to gain a better understanding of the text.

In verses 6-8 Jesus moves downward to the cross, while in verses 9-11 he moves upward to exaltation. We can call these bi-directional movements that are Christo-eschatological: Jesus' incarnation, cross, and exaltation are manifestations of God's *establishing* his rule in the universe. When it arrives in full, the ultimate result will be every knee bowing, willingly or unwillingly, and every tongue confessing that Jesus Christ is Lord.

We must be attuned to the fact that this paragraph is not a systematic theology attempting to encompass every aspect of God's salvific rule. For example, it says nothing about Christ's death for us. Why is this the case? I think it is because Paul's interest at this point is elsewhere. Instead of showing believers the meaning of these things for their lives, the apostle is interested in how they apply to Christ himself. Paul draws out the significance of this for Christians by way of an interchange based on the surrounding ethical sections in verses 1-4 and verses 12-16. The model of Christ in verses 6-11 aims to show a relationship between believers' conduct and actions and the conduct and actions of Christ Jesus himself.

In verse 5 we should understand that Paul is exhorting believers to adopt the same relational attitude toward each other that was found in Christ Jesus. In other words, their frame of mind should be modeled after his. The apostle seems to be writing about believers' "conformity" to Christ, not exclusively their "imitation" of him.

At the outset of verses 6-8, it is clear that Christ Jesus shared equality with God, but did not use this to his own advantage. Verse 6 speaks of Christ sharing God's glory (John 17:5; Hebrews 1:3), his divinity, majesty and splendor. The second part of verse 6 requires additional clarification if we are to better understand the text. Some translations use the unhelpful wording, "did not consider equality with God *something to be grasped,*" which makes it sound like Christ is grasping at something that he does not have or does not realize he already has.

The point here is found elsewhere. Christ does not view equality as a shield against death, even death on the cross. Equality, in this case, relates to "giving" not "receiving." Christ does not view being equal with God as something to take advantage of or to use in his own favor.

In verse 7 we encounter the strong adversative "but" or "instead" he [Christ] voluntarily empties himself of his rights by taking the form of a servant/slave and being born like other humans. Note here that slavery in Jesus' cultural context can refer to a loss of one's rights.

As Christ Jesus empties himself, he does not entirely set aside his divinity, but allows and embraces the incarnation. He becomes a slave and identifies with the human race through becoming part of it. The next sentence gives further affirmation of this. Christ was found to be a man; he appeared before others as a human being.

In 2:8 we have the climax of the first part of the paragraph. The up-to-down movement is now completed and reaches its climax in Christ's horrific death on the cross. Christ Jesus humbles himself, choosing the path of obedience all the way to death—to the extremity of death on the cross. Christ's death was not that of human necessity, but that of divine initiative. The death he died was the most humiliating and degrading within his cultural context.

Here we see that Christ's *humility* and *obedience* are to be a mark of the Christian attitude to life. In seeing something of the action of Christ as related to these two central elements of the first part of the paragraph, Christians are to have the same frame of mind as their prime example, Christ Jesus.

A radical change now takes place. Christ has been the subject of the main verbs in verses 6-8, but now in verses 9-11, God the Father becomes the subject of these verbs. Christ's movement is now upward from death to exaltation.

This change is clearly marked by the "therefore" in verse 9 and the whole of verses 9-11. Christ's exaltation should not to be considered a reward, because the movement of verses 6-8 compels us to think of Jesus' whole life as one of humble obedience—not merit or compensation.

As a result of God's grace towards him, Christ is vindicated. We need to be careful here not to turn his humility/exaltation into a principle of some kind of divine law for all. The principle is there (humility), and the movement is there (exaltation), but the focus in this context is on what happens to Christ himself.

In verse 9 God exalts Christ to the highest place: the place of incomparability to all others. God graciously confers upon him the name above all names. I suggest it is better to see this name only implied here, but made explicit in verse 11 as "Lord", not Jesus. Verses 10 and 11 seem to affirm this with, "in order that in honor of the name which belongs to Jesus every knee shall bow in heaven, earth and the world below and confess that he is Lord to the glory of God the Father." Christ's exaltation as Lord brings with it the claim of a universal Lordship.

This last verse, an echo of Isaiah 45:18-23, raises an important tension and is useful for us to refer to:

"Turn to me and be saved, all you ends of the earth;

for I am God, and there is no other.

By myself I have sworn, my mouth has uttered in all integrity a word that will not be revoked: Before me every knee will bow; by me every tongue will swear. . . ."

Where is the tension here in the Isaiah passage? God is presently Lord—there is no other (verses 18, 22). And it is on this basis that we have a call to salvation *now* (verse 22). At the same time, there is a universal proclamation of God's Lordship (verse 23), that is yet to be established. The tension exists here in Isaiah, as well as in Philippians. Christ's exaltation has already taken place, and he has received the name *Lord*. However, we have not yet seen every knee bow or every tongue confess, and therein lies the tension.

141

There is the double focus of eschatology (the day of Christ) and Christology again being woven together here. Christians are exhorted to be living spirituality with bowed knees (this relates intrinsically to verses 1-4 and verses 12-16) as they, in the present, practice what is sure to take place in the future.

The bowing of the knee and the confessing of the tongue by all is not necessarily voluntary. In some cases, there will be a forced submission to a greater power, and "all those who have raged against him will be put to shame" (Isa. 45:24).

Philippians 2:12-13: Continuing

(12) Therefore, my dear friends, as you have always obeyed—not only in my presence, but now much more in my absence—continue to work out your salvation with fear and trembling, (13) for it is God who works in you to will and to act according to his good purpose.

Our closing section begins in verse 12 with another, "Therefore." In other words, the apostle is drawing together much of what we have read previously. Paul addresses the Philippians with, "my dear friends," showing us again the intimate relationship he had with this community of Christians.

The exhortation here is picked up from verses 5-11 and expressed in part b of verse 12. At this juncture, we need to remember that the exhortation is based on the divine example of the pre-existent and incarnate Christ.

In verse 12a, the apostle first writes about their obedience from the time they first heard and received the gospel. Their problem is not necessarily obedience.

In verse 12b, Paul exhorts them to continue to work out their salvation with fear and trembling. Like the Philippians, our problem is that we often get stuck right here. We lose the path and begin to seek out alternatives that inevitably lead us astray.

142

The Philippians appear to have totally, or at least substantially, lost their joy in Christ. Paul may not come to visit them, and they are facing the threat of external opposition and the danger of internal disintegration. Unlike the Philippians, we are not waiting for Paul, but we do face the plight of oppositions and disintegrations. How are we to live in the midst of these pressures? A clear indication of living spirituality follows.

Paul challenges them: "continue" to work out your salvation. What might the apostle mean here? This *continue* may present a question for some of us. If Christians are already saved, why are they being exhorted to work out their salvation?

My assessment is that there is a massive difference between bringing about and working out something that already exists. In this context, salvation is not merely *justification* (accepting Christ as Messiah and being declared holy) as we usually assume, but it includes the whole eschatological process of *sanctification* (being made holy).

Here's the point—our salvation already exists, just as was the case for the Philippians. Paul confirms that neither we nor they have brought this about. Remember, God is the one who begins a good work (1:6) and will carry it through to completion. Does this mean that Christians are to be on *cruise control* spirituality and expect God to take care of everything? No, it does not. Cruise control equates spiritual impoverishment. God does promise to be at work in our lives, but at the same time, we are to pursue the whole breadth of salvation—to go after it with all we have, to live it in a manner worthy of the gospel (1:27).

Notice that this working out of salvation is to be done with *fear* and *trembling*. These two words, used together in the Scripture only by Paul, are likely to refer to the seriousness of the matter at hand. Christians have a responsibility to work out their salvation with awe and reverence for God, and as we see in verse 13, it is God who is at work in them.

It seems to me that Paul presents us with a nuanced and balanced perspective. We are called to pursue salvation: the whole eschatological process up to and including the *day of Christ*. But we must remember that this neither means that we bring it about, nor that we are solely responsible to accomplish it. Let's again be aware of the either/or fallacy in this context. E*ither* "I do nothing" *or* "I do it all" leads us astray.

Such extremes make it easy to lose the path and hard to live the Christian life: living spirituality. The apostle used the words, "Fear and Trembling," because it is indeed an awesome, even frightful thing, to have the Almighty God at work in our lives. We are not on our own and cannot solely take credit for completing the task ourselves. Being dependent on God, on the other hand, renders us responsible for contributing to our sanctification. And God wants it that way.

14

Losing and Finding the Path

The truth that God is at work in us, while a marvel, is no assurance that we won't make wrong choices, ignore key map markers, or otherwise get ourselves lost. Losing and finding the path is a central issue for living spirituality. When we get lost, God in his mercy promises to lead us back and to help us find the path again.

Here in the Alps some days are crystal clear, which makes path finding on the journey relatively easy. But when the cold north wind blows, *la bise* in French, it can bring with it a fog so thick that it's difficult at times not to lose the path. The gray, wispy clouds waft in and then out. Sometimes they block the way ahead completely, other times they obscure it, making the visibility different from one moment to the next. Community with God— living spirituality—can be like that.

Tom's story

Tom was unaware that he had a serious problem when he came to Swiss L'Abri. He was a disciple of Jesus and on the path to life, but also prone to the legalism taught in his church. Tom was entering the fog. He had started well, but fell into making up lists, personal rituals, codes, and regimes, assuming that these defined spirituality.

His life began to revolve around a legalistic regimen of *do this and don't do that.*

He had embraced the assumption that if he did what he was "supposed" to do, everything would fall into place. His lists, systems, and codes became God. He was following idols, instead of loving God, being in community with him. Tom's focus was leading him astray.

Legalism left Tom cold, hard, and judgmental. Furthermore, without realizing it, he was ignoring his own sin. Tom put others into boxes and left them there, showing no mercy or love. They were not good Christians or good people because they were not following Tom's statutes and regulations—they weren't like him. He thought he was better than others, and therefore they didn't deserve his concern or attention. But then he found that nothing was falling into place as expected. He lamented, *Why oh God, doesn't it all go as it should? I'm doing my part, yet you don't seem to be paying attention.*

Tom's external edifice began to crack and disintegrate, at least inwardly. During his stay in the L'Abri community, he faced challenges to his legalism and to his lack of attention to his own sin. Tom knew something about the need for redemption in Christ, but somehow his legalistic structure had begun to obstruct his visibility of it. Eventually, he experienced an identity crisis. Tom was caught between who he should be and who he was. His lack of deep personal community with God, through faith in Christ and in the power of the Spirit, became increasingly evident.

When this took place, Tom turned toward what he assumed was his only other option. He thought that since the lists, codes, and regimes failed, he should abandon them all and just do what he wanted. In rejection of legalism, all that was left was freedom. Tom now let it all go. There was no reason to hold onto anything. He went from creating and following rules, to breaking them all. Life became one big party.

Instead of following the map, Tom had attempted to *make it up as he went along* which resulted in a sterile legalism or living as he pleased. Either of these perspectives guarantees failure. Tom was lost and utterly falling apart. His breakdown would prove to be a good thing, because it began to lead him out of the fog.

As I previously pointed out, this type of false-option syndrome is evident in many people's lives. Tom's life is a good example of how the extreme legalism often found in Christian circles frequently brings about the opposite response of extreme freedom. While it is true that living spirituality cannot be reduced to a *list* mentality, neither can it be a wholesale *freedom* to choose any way of life that we please. Both of these result in impoverished spirituality.

What was Tom's real option? To begin to move in a new direction it was crucial for him to return to the map of Scripture. In doing so, Tom discovered that it is not God's law that is a problem. The Ten Commandments are still relevant and crucial for living as the people of God today. Further, Romans 7 affirms that God's law is holy and good. And ultimately significant is Jesus' teaching to his followers in Matthew 22:37-40 that the two greatest commandments are to love God with all that you are, and to love your neighbor as yourself.

For Tom to reverse his impoverished spirituality it was mandatory for him to see that living spirituality is rooted in something far deeper: community with God, through Christ, in the power of the Spirit. This leads to a new way of life and embracing the worldview of Scripture in all that it comprises.

As a result of this new direction, Tom found himself undergoing the dynamic transformation of desire. This meant not to *make it up as he went along*, but to follow the crucified and risen One, and to have the law written on his heart so that he might seek, in Christ and through the power of the Spirit, to serve God and others.

147

When we reflect on this story and its application we can see that such service can be done in a myriad of ways: from feeding the poor, to offering shelter for the seeker who is weary and oppressed; from being an artist or poet, to being a doctor or nurse; from calculating figures, to preserving the planet. The possibilities of service are numerous and unending.

Redeeming Memories

Let's now look at another example of how we can lose our direction. Most of us struggle with how to view certain past circumstances, and we often misunderstand how we should perceive them. The result is spiritual impoverishment.

In your past, you may have experienced abuse, suffering, shame, guilt, and pain; or pride, being the center of attention, and self-sufficiency. Memories may haunt or revive you—but either of these outcomes may contribute to losing the path. If you are always returning to your past and reliving pain or vanity, then you are following your own map, and not God's.

Here's the point. You may be prone to living in and being obsessed by your past. You may assume that the burden or blessing of such a past is what identifies who you are in the present. If you are caught living in this past, as if it is all that you have, you are giving your past a much greater place in your life than it should have.

How do you live with your memories and what perspective are you to have toward them? What are you to do with all the wonderful or horrible things that you did to others, that were done to you, or that you did to yourself? Are you not now the same person you were in those moments?

If we aren't careful, our present life becomes merely one of remembering. We spend a good deal of time re-viewing our pasts. Remembering is important, but when the past dominates the present to such a degree that it potentially controls who we are, it becomes a problem. To prevent that, we are well advised to understand what role the past plays in living spirituality in the present. Otherwise, our yesterdays end up *entirely* identifying our today. Let me explain further.

When we are down, we try to build ourselves up by looking back to previous exploits. Remember our great high school team? We won the championship that year—we are still amazing. Or when we are up, we tear ourselves down by looking back to previous failures. Remember that broken relationship? If we failed once, we'll surely fail again. And there may even be times when we find ourselves doing a bit of both in order to avoid dealing with the present.

To move in a different direction, I suggest that we reflect on the past with a present-redemptive memory. You are a Christian, and this means that with a redemptive perspective, the past identifies less and less of who you are. Being a Christian creates a new identity for you, and from the point of conversion on, you should begin to deal with the past in another way. To understand your identity, it is essential to understand that your redemption in Christ now provides your primary outlook for the present. From that ever-present perspective, you see everything else.

While it is true that you cannot ignore the past, it is also true that its power to control your present should diminish. Although memories of an unredeemed past do not entirely disappear, they begin to lose their power to create your present identity. A raging battle may ensue as they fight for a dominant position within you, but other priorities will begin to gradually overshadow the memories that previously controlled your identity. As you experience your redemptive memory of conversion, these priorities will include loving God, following Christ, engaging the Spirit and culture, giving thanks, diminishing sin, avoiding idolatry, and serving others. These characteristics, rather than the patterns that marked your unredeemed past, will begin to identify who you are now.

Being redeemed has power for the triad of your past, present, and future. Because you are a new creation in Christ, this redemption extends to the whole view of your life. The redemption brought about by the crucified and risen One and its present impact, touches all of who you are now—your past and future included. Such a new perspective releases you from the false identity of destructive patterns that condemn, or euphoric patterns that produce pride and arrogance. Instead of accepting this release, many people struggle with holding onto false identities, which amounts to role playing and giving a performance. And this too results in losing the path. Let's look at Jenny's story to illustrate how this manifests itself.

Jenny's story

Jenny was a Christian. She knew that she was saved by Christ and that God loved her. Prior to becoming a Christian, severe struggles with a sense of betrayal and abandonment had been with her for years. Her life had been plagued by failed relationships, where the line between love and sex had been blurred beyond recognition, leaving her with very low self-esteem and a lack of self-worth.

There is, of course, more to this story that is important to understand. Jenny's parents had shown her little love or compassion. They often condemned her for who she was and for never measuring up to their standards. She never could do enough to please them or to gain their approval. Furthermore, they told Jenny that she was worthless and made sure that she felt shame and guilt, because God was against her. Although she had accepted something of her parents' evaluation in theory, Jenny remained suspicious of its complete accuracy. She rebelled against them, but in ways that tended to make matters worse. Jenny was acting as if she was worthless, not as if she truly had worth and value.

Through her rebellion against her parents, Jenny was really screaming *I do have worth.* What she had learned in becoming a Christian was important. Her rebellion was a good thing—it was against something wrong. She did have intrinsic worth as an image of God, and it was right to rebel against her parents' abuse, erroneous condemnation, and false standards.

God was on her side and affirmed her when she rebelled against the deception she faced. At the same time, God also critiqued her for the inappropriate ways she went about this. Jenny could see that her rebellion and its inappropriate manifestations could be separated. One was right, while the other was not.

In becoming a Christian, Jenny experienced substantial healing in these areas of her difficult past and understood that she was redeemed. Still, after a period of time her memories of guilt, fear of rejection, and lack of self worth grew in power and influence and she began to lose her way. These weighty experiences haunted her present life and had corrosive effects on her faith. When this happened, Jenny was devastated. She saw herself as caught in the web of all her previous problems and that these identified her.

At this point, it was imperative that Jenny embrace a redemptive memory. While she could not magically make her sinful past and her parents' harmful deceptions disappear, it was crucial for her to recognize that it was God who validated her and that she was his child. God would not abandon her or require her to measure up to false standards. God would not deceive her and he would not betray her.

Redemptive memory was deeply connected with her conversion to Christ and to sanctification. This had never occurred to Jenny when the flood of the apparently unredeemed past engulfed her. By following the map in the power of the Spirit and entering into transformation, Jenny had to realize that she was not alone. God was faithfully at work in her and would gently help her find the path again. She stood before him in the present as washed and cleansed by the blood of the crucified and risen One, and all that

151

had happened in her life was redeemed by Christ—everything from failed relationships, low self-esteem, and parental abuse, to her wrong ways of rebelling. Jenny was no longer enslaved to the past and its control of her life in the present. She was free in Christ to live her new identity.

When we ignore the map, which directs and marks out our journey, we may fail to see the extraordinary truth that the apostle Paul wrote in Romans: "But God demonstrates his own love for us in this: While we were still sinners Christ died for us." And "Therefore, there is now no condemnation for those who are in Christ Jesus" (5:8; 8:1).

Living spirituality is not a dress rehearsal. It is the real thing. Living in God's world in God's way means that our pasts are redeemed and that we are released to live in the present, and the future, possessing a new identity. Memories of sin will remain, but the power of redemption begins to trace over our enslavement to the past and frees us to live as children of God in the now. As we are welcomed into community with God, our lives begin to reflect this reality because we live on the basis of our new identity in Christ. The tracing over that redemption provides is one of the many beauties and blessings of a life that is increasingly aligned with the Infinite One, whose view of time is not linear or limited like ours. Even when our visibility is clouded by sin, God will help us find the path when we lose it.

15

Love and Community

The next crucial issue before us is how we are to love and live in community with each other. These two realities of living spirituality are sometimes those that seem far from identifying us and our churches. We need to focus on reversing our impoverishment because love and community are at the heart of the Christian life.

I grew up in the once famous Haight-Ashbury neighborhood in the heart of San Francisco. During the 1960s and 70s, masses of people flocked to this part of the city from all over the world. What attracted all these people? What were they searching for? How are we to read the times back then?

One striking development was the oft-repeated slogan *turn on, tune in, and drop out.* This was radical stuff. Among other things, it meant taking drugs, unmasking the superficial, and rejecting a society built on greed, money, and possessions. The slogan suggested trying a new way—living for love, freedom, and getting high. Many came to San Francisco to rebel against the "buy, sell, produce, and consume" culture that threatened to turn people into machines. They were seeking to leave behind that which was seen as hypocritical and impersonal. And they also came hoping to find love and real humanness.

San Francisco was *the* place in the world to be—the place where it was all happening. It was in the papers, on TV, and soon on tourist itineraries. I remember being at the first Human-Be-In in Golden Gate Park with thousands of others. Plenty was happening—books, music, poetry, drugs. The city turned into the wild adventure it represented: changing the world and creating a utopian community that would live together in love as it should.

One of the things that the San Francisco of the 1960s was renowned for was this heightened emphasis on love. We even changed the name of Haight Street to Love Street. People said that love was in the San Francisco air, and something of that was true. Despite the protests against the war in Vietnam, appeals against the lack of civil rights, and resistance against the oppression of government, love always remained a relevant concern and a central issue.

In those days, the city had free clinics for people with medical needs, free care for the abused and battered, free shelter for the homeless, free food for the hungry, and free concerts in Golden Gate park. Ideal? Utopia? Yes, perhaps for a moment. But only a waning moment which was far from perfect—though it was an authentic effort made by some to truly care for others. All of this was set in a community searching for reality and a deeper meaning to life, and which attempted in some way to reach out in love to a world of indifference and greed.

But after a while the streets got rougher, drug abuse proliferated, and things began to get ugly. Returning from the free rock concert at Altamont speedway near San Francisco, I remember thinking that the love the 1960s stood for was fading and had become illusory.

Altamont was a catastrophe. Violence exploded and there was killing. That night marked the beginning of the end of the vision for a new world consisting of a caring and loving community. The heartfelt cry and one of the leading slogans of the day—*all you need is love*—failed, and failed miserably. "Buy, sell, produce, and consume" returned with overwhelming force. Marketing and financial security re-emerged and became central. And for many, money once again became the dominating, yet illusive god that they thought would lead them to freedom and love.

I am not saying that what began in San Francisco had nothing unique or special about it. There was a striking outpouring of love. But, when love has no basis or personal referent outside of ourselves—notably the Infinite One who *is* love—we are left to make it up as we go along. And as we attempt this, there will be serious consequences of breakdown and dysfunction. Love, when not anchored in and referring to the personal God, has limited significance and meaning.

Several other problems led to the demise of the 1960s' version of love. The movement didn't take into account the truth that people are sinful, that love is not whatever we make it to be, that idealism and utopias will be unsustainable, and that a journey needs a destination. We lacked direction, and though we shared some common ground, it was insufficient, because it offered no basis or referent for love that might hold things together.

Illuminated by Love

By contrast, the map of Scripture directs us to a sustainable love and a realistic freedom. True freedom and true love are our key markers, as they are anchored in the personal God who has graciously offered us his revelation. We are on a creational and redeeming Spirit-powered journey that is going somewhere and towards someone. The map points out and takes into account our sin and our need for direction toward *who* love is and *what* love looks like. The map of Scripture gives us the path to follow. It is the path to life, illuminated by God who is love.

Unlike the *make it up as you go along* love of the 1960s San Francisco, this mapped-out truth shows that the Infinite One is love. The origin and source of love is God. Amidst Father, Son, and

155

Spirit there is a community of love that existed before the creation of the world.

This community reaches out to us in love through creation, covenant, and the nation of Israel—through poet, sage, and prophet. And then, love is made flesh as the Father sends the Son on a mission on his behalf. The Son inaugurates the Kingdom of God, and part of the mission is accomplished. Yet as death threatens, Satan begins to be defeated and resurrection triumphs. The crucified One lives so that we too might have the destiny of love and life. And then the Spirit comes to reside with us on the journey: to represent the love, life, and power of both the Father and the Son until the end of the age.

Engraved by Love

The New Testament mapping clearly highlights that God is love and that Christians are to love God and each other. Loving your neighbor as yourself, loving your enemies, and loving others— these actions should identify those who follow the crucified and risen One. Notice that self-love is all together appropriate in the context of being loved by God: *love your neighbor as yourself.* But outside this context, love easily becomes corrupted, untrustworthy, and selfish. However, God's love for us and our proper love for ourselves can help us to open up possibilities of having greater love for others.

Love is to shine through, not only in meeting people where they are and giving accurate answers to those who are seeking, but it must also to be visible when generational, racial, and cultural differences cause division. Our destination of being transformed into the image of Christ requires nothing less.

To be more specific, open your Bible and reflect on John 13:34. You will see that Jesus leaves his disciples with a new commandment: love. His followers are to love one another as he has loved them. The pathway to life is powerfully illuminated—

Christians are to treat each other the way they have been treated by Jesus. This includes washing feet, repentance, releasing and healing, breaking away from inauthenticity, and being willing to express a genuine concern for others through serving them. As far as this path is from our consumer-driven, self-centered, superficial culture, this is love.

Those who follow the crucified and risen One are to grow increasingly aware that love is engraved on them and it is etched into the depths of their souls. It should be the imprint that produces Christian unity and identifies us to the watching world. When people look at us, they are to see our love for each other and the unity that results from this.

John 17:20-23 makes this directive abundantly clear. Our unity and community, like that of the Father and Son, has an impact on the world. This unity is one of the central features that make it possible for the world to know that the Father sent Jesus, and that he loves us. A scriptural mapping confirms that this is the path to life and that these are the chief characteristics by which the unbelieving world will recognize that we are in community with God and true disciples of Jesus.

A Lack of Love

As Christians, we have expressed this love and unity poorly. We have been unloving to those seeking by not giving honest answers to honest questions, and we have not shown enough love to our brothers and sisters in Christ to have unity wherever it can be found. As disciples of the crucified and risen One, we are acting as if there is no engraving, no imprint, as if we have not been loved by Jesus, and as if the Father has not sent the Son. Lamentably, we are missing the mark of a Christian: failing to truly love others and to be unified. This is deplorable.

Growing numbers of Christians and non-Christians are bewildered by a sense of the inauthenticity and the lack of real and genuine love among us. The words fake, arrogant, and aloof all too often describe and characterize us, both inside and outside the Christian community.

Believers become apathetic and cynical. They're floundering and drifting. Unbelievers look and say, "Who cares." There's nothing different in the Christian community. Then, these unbelieving observers turn away and go about business as usual. And all the while we are consumed with constructing our Christian bowling alleys and health clubs, dogmatically privileging our doctrines over people, constructing our apologetics without love, chasing after making more money, or performing in the theater of being cool. *Living* love and unity gets left behind in the shadows.

Where is the true Christian response of costly love? Where have we lovingly given answers to a lost culture and comforted the souls who are trapped within it? What has happened to following the crucified and risen One in the Christianity of our own day?

Renewing Love

Deep spiritual renewal is necessary, even vital, if we are to reverse spiritual impoverishment. There are no simple formulas, no superficial solutions. Through the power of the Spirit, an informed holistic, interactive, interpretative, theological, redemptive spirituality lived in community with God, with the map in hand for the journey, renewal can begin to take place. Christ's love is to flow through us and then out of us to each other, our neighbors, our enemies, all people, and creation. This regeneration translates into a greater expression of that love which is engraved on and etched deep into our hearts. We are to be so filled by this love that it overflows out of us towards others. Christian love in action is powerful and life-changing.

If we are to reverse spiritual impoverishment and high ambiguity, we must live the answers that lead us into the community that God has given us. And this means seeing love and unity as central to our own communities, while also offering something persuasive and dynamic to the watching world. Our hearts, minds, and the whole of our lives are to demonstrate this love and unity which testifies to the truth that the Son was sent by the Father. In spite of brokenness and sin there exists something real, genuine, and substantial that brings forth the wonder and reality that God is with us.

As I pointed out earlier, we who are Christians are in community with Father, Son and Spirit. This community is profound, rich, spiritual, redemptive, and life-giving. It is this reality that is meant to shape and form our lifetimes in community with each other and the world. God loves us and we are to love each other. That means those in the Christian community in particular and all humans in general. It's a massive task, yet it is our command and our calling. There is no better way.

For all of us who follow Christ the mandate is clear. Love as you have been loved by the crucified and risen One. Christians need to learn to appreciate each other's practical and social differences instead of comparing or degrading them. We are not to force others to be like us or to do it our way because our way is always the right way. Love is not a forced formula of turning others into copies of ourselves, nor a book of rules or a cultural program. It comes from above and concerns us all. Love is personal. And it is to be lived in community.

True Community

There is an acute and desperate need for creating genuine and authentic Christian communities. Churches exist in abundance, but many thinking people today are fleeing them, sitting on the sidelines, about to give up. Searching and perceptive Christians are becoming refugees in what should be the land of the living, but which no longer offers anything worth living for. When buildings, programs, and events replace people, we are losing the path.

159

In order to reverse our spiritual impoverishment we need God's help. It is imperative to move in new directions. Our churches ought to first be true communities. People are the priority. Hospitality, love, and forgiveness are to stand out, and our communities should be places of alluring grace. Christian communities are not to be other-worldly, but to be *this*-worldly. We are to be down-to-earth. We are to share life together. We are to be real people, living in the real world, and doing real things And Christ is to be Lord of it all—of all life.

①NEEDS
CLARITY
STATEMENT
TOD
AMBIGUOUS

Others come first—through washing feet, laying down lives, loving as Jesus has loved us. This extends to all we say and do as we live in this wild, wonderful, and broken world as broken people. Our actions will never be perfect, but nevertheless we are to continue to seek to demonstrate love in the midst of sin. This is living spirituality, as it will result in further transformation into the image of Christ and diminishing spiritual impoverishment.

Another crucial factor for true community is that we teach relevant, interesting, and insightful map-reading skills. There are more and more Bibles and more and more translations, but we have little encouragement and direction as to how to read the map—this precious word, this Word of God. This is not just a pastor's, a scholar's, or seminary student's task, but it is the responsibility of all Christians. We have, generally speaking, become unskilled and illiterate map readers, and this is bound to carry with it grave consequences for our spirituality and our communities.

Many, many times, those who claim to be the most biblical among us are more interested in dogmatically protecting their particular interpretations, rather than carefully studying, contemplating, and being open to the map's direction—a direction they claim to hold so dear. *Whatever the map means to me is what it means* has widespread influence today, and this lack of biblical understanding can and does create serious problems for love and unity.

160

If there is no community, no teaching, and no interest in developing good map reading skills, then we lose the path and will die. The unreal, impersonal, and dying should not characterize us. Such a portrayal of Christianity is not accurate, is not of God, is not following the map, is not the path to life, and is certainly not the journey of living spirituality.

True communities will refuse to practice a narrow sectarianism by engaging in a variety of levels of intense map reading *and* interaction with culture. Exhibiting the imprint of love should be dramatically specific to who we are and what we do. May God grant us map reading skills and careful contemplation that leads to renewal, along with cautious and wise participation in our cultures for the sake of creation, for Christ, and for love.

As we seek to follow the map and to be living spirituality, our communities should be those that listen, speak the truth in love, are open to dialogue, and are well informed biblically, spiritually, and culturally. Our spirituality is living and to be lived, because it is connected to the source and origin of spirituality: Father, Son and Spirit. This intimate connection provides us with authentic community that can begin to reflect the true community we are to have with each other, and to live out in the world as we seek through the redemption of Christ, in the power of the Spirit, to bring praise to God.

Part Four
The End of the Journey:
A New Beginning

16

Our Destiny and Destination

After having explored crucial issues that illuminate the path for living spirituality, we now come to the end of the journey. No doubt, there will be many parts of the journey that we will travel again and again, but our destiny is ultimately to be found in a new beginning. Our hope and confidence are located in the truth that the journey is indeed going somewhere.

Destiny

Destiny is one of the key driving forces behind living spirituality. By looking at it and orienting ourselves toward it, we can see where we are and where we are going. What is our destiny?

Turning to the map and guide again, we see that the apostle Paul tells us that to be disciples of the crucified and risen One—to be living spirituality—means to be transformed into the image of Christ (Romans 8:29; 1 Cor. 15:49; 2 Cor. 3:18; Col. 3:10). That is our destiny—a transformation from death to life. And this comes from Christ and the Spirit. *Rejoice and be glad in it.*

John's letter affirms a similar direction: the Father has given us such a love that allows us to be children of God now. Though we don't yet know what we will be like, we know that when the Christ is revealed we will be *like* him (1 John 3:2).

Notice that both these writers are careful to maintain the reality of relation and distinction. They write of us being *transformed* into Christ's image and that we will be *like* him. When we reach our destiny, relation and distinction will not disappear or be collapsed into each other. Paul and John clearly point us to the truth that we are and will become like Christ, but they also stress that we will not be Christ.

Our present community with God is leading us further into a deeper and more intimate community in the future. And for true community to exist, then and now, there is relation and distinction. Sin eventually will be wiped away and renewal completed. As Christ has life and images God and because he is our representative, we too will live and image God as Christ does.

For those who are Christians, the journey has begun. We are in motion, transition, translation, and moving in this direction. In some manner we are already imaging Christ because we are children of God; he is the firstborn of many from every tribe, language, people, and nation. Conformity and transformation should be a present reality within us in an ever-increasing way from the time we become Christians to the day we see God face to face. Nothing could be more glorious and loving than this marvelous destiny.

Many people today lack direction and claim to have no destination. For them, only the journey counts. This is not the case for Christians. We are going to image the crucified and risen One and therefore we will live forever in the age to come. In order to reverse spiritual impoverishment and to diminish ambiguity, this present and its future reality must be prominently configured into the whole of our lives now. Transformed into the image of Christ? Indeed. The thought of it, the reality of it, the audacity and magnitude of it are staggering. God's grace should strike us as everlastingly astonishing. *Stop and reflect on your destiny.*

The journey of this book now comes to its conclusion, but that of Scripture will go on forever. For our part, we started by surveying the landscape and observing that high ambiguity leads us away from a living spirituality that is holistic, interactive, interpretative, theological, and redemptive. As we prepared to travel, we kept in mind the importance of reversing spiritual impoverishment.

Then we opened the map of Scripture and, with the guide of the Holy Spirit, looked at the importance of relation and distinction in terms of the good Creator and what he created. We reminded ourselves that our referent is the God who is there and that living spirituality is deeply connected to creation. We saw that brokenness and sin require redemption, that the covenant and the arrival of the Messiah and the Kingdom of God illuminate the path for the journey, and that there is a tension in living spirituality within the already and not yet.

As we moved further into the journey, we focused more closely on specific sections of the map to understand that grace reigns and sin matters, and that we are redeemed and are not to live self-focused lives, but are to love one another. Then we looked at justification and sanctification and what it means to be and become holy and how that works out in degrees.

We realized that we are incapable of exhaustive knowledge even though we have been given sufficient knowledge to know that God is there. We faced adversity and losing the path—but also finding it again. Looking at love and community, we saw that we need renewal to reverse our spiritual impoverishment and highlighted that the central call is for us to love each other as God has loved us. This can begin with our community of Father, Son and Spirit. From that union, and in our connection with others who children of God, we are being transformed into the image of Christ.

Where the Journey Finally Leads

We now arrive at our final destination: a renewed heaven and earth. Consider this as both the end of the journey and its beginning at the same time. This is where the journey will ultimately take us and where we will be forever. Theologically, God as creator and redeemer sets the parameters and gives the basis for this view. The map affirms that God will bring about a renewed creation at the end of the age.

God's post-flood covenant with *all* creation (Gen. 9) and the incarnation, life, death, and resurrection of Christ show us that *all* creation will be redeemed from sin and evil (Rm. 8; 1 Cor. 15). To dwell on the renewed earth means that God the Creator will redeem what is his and all that passes through the refining fire of judgment will be restored and made new.

There will be relation and distinction with what was before and what comes after. God's way into the next age is neither absolute continuity nor absolute discontinuity. The judgment of grace will not destroy the earth, but will purify and cleanse it to the glory of God. For God's aim is not destruction, but transformation. He will be faithful to creation and will redeem it through the crucified and risen One.

Our destination has an earthbound perspective and this is highly relevant to living spirituality. As Paul points out in his letter to Timothy, everything that God has created is good (1 Tim 4:1-5). Creational spirituality remains significant, and it has a place not only in living spirituality in the present, but it has far reaching meaning for the future. Reversing spiritual impoverishment is dependent on a growing awareness that, in the midst of the brokenness and sin, God already—through Christ—restores that which he made, and he will do so completely at the end of time. This radical truth illuminates the path for our present lives— creation has been and will always be God's handiwork.

We are given a vital mandate to resist the disfiguration of creation and to stand against all oppression and injustice towards it. After all, creation is God's and we are to enable it to praise him. Whether we are talking about oil spills, global warming, deforestation, or violations of human rights, God calls us to be accountable now. Our future destination is to be a feature of the present that is to have an impact on the journey itself.

If we say we love God, but turn around and destroy creation, we are living a severe contradiction. If we reduce creation to the simply mechanistic or impersonal we are failing to love what God has made. When we fail to love creation, we fail to love humans and we risk losing our focus on the truth that all, including humanity, are part of the created. Such a loss would inevitably mean we are denying the Creator and Redeemer.

When our worldview assumes that everything is headed for destruction we tend to reject the worth and value of God's creation. It becomes misused and misunderstood, depleted, and torn apart. All manners of disfiguration blot out creation's capacity to praise God. Some Christians believe that destruction is God's way with the created, so what does it matter? Go ahead and let it go. It's all headed for the flames anyway. Yet this is not the case. The intensity of redemption burns into transformation already now and ultimately at the end of the age. In this way, creation can give praise to the Infinite personal One who created it, attaining its final and glorious destiny.

As Christians we are destined to be with God when all is renewed. In the future when this is accomplished, we will inhabit a restored earth, living in the presence of God in all his glory.

Visions of this outlook appear in many places throughout the Scripture, but are especially vivid in Revelation 21-22 where John writes of seeing a new heaven and earth. Let's take a closer look at what is written in these chapters—the end of the journey and its beginning.

What John sees is a fulfillment of Isaiah 65:17 and 66:22. There will be a new heaven and a new earth and no longer any sea, which may relate to the thought that the sea was a place of evil. John sees the Holy city. New Jerusalem descends out of heaven from God. The city has at least four characteristics; it is holy, it is new, it descends out of heaven, and it is from God. There is a marked and radical contrast with what is old in this marvelous, awe-inspiring vision. All the images used are meant to strike us—to make us take notice of what God is going to do (21:1-2).

There is then a proclamation from the throne. God himself will dwell with his people. This statement refers back to the Old Testament when God's dwelling place was the ark and later the temple. It is also affirmed by the New Testament in the person of Christ, and through the Spirit in the church—but now God's presence with us will be entirely visible and reach completion.

The distance we now experience in community with God will be obliterated and completely transformed. He will wipe away our tears. In direct community with God, there will be no more death, mourning, crying or pain. God himself will comfort, heal and redeem his people. The old order of things has passed away; the new will have completed its consummation (21:3-4).

He who was seated on the throne says, "I am making everything new." In renewal, we are not offered an escape, but an engagement with heaven and earth—the material world where matter and spirit will meet in visible ways. We need to recall and re-affirm that there is already a present aspect of this newness in our lives as Christians. If we are in Christ, we are new creations. However, notice that God's salvific activity includes the political, social, economic and the creation itself. John is instructed to write this down as it is trustworthy and true (21:5).

God affirms to John, "It is done" or better, "They are done" referring to all the events to take place up to and including the restoration of all things. God is the Alpha and Omega. He is the beginning and the end. There is no beginning before God and he is the end of everything in the sense that all things will end up before him.

Those that are thirsty are given the water of life and it is the one who overcomes who will be rewarded and inherit the blessings of God and share in his rule. Those who overcome are reassured that God will be their God and that they will be his children. They are then contrasted with the cowardly—those in this context who have not been willing to suffer or perhaps even die for their faith in Christ, and unbelievers—who are likely to be those who have renounced their faith in Christ in the midst of persecution, and the vile, the murderers, the sexually immoral, those who practice magic arts, the idolaters, and the liars. In contrast to the inheritance of those who overcome, these will not have a place in the new heaven and earth; they are destined to the lake of fire, the second death (21:6-8).

An angel, one of the seven, shows John in the Spirit, the Holy city. The city is said to shine with the glory of God, signifying his real presence. In reference to this radiance, John speaks of it as "like" precious stones. Glistening as a valued jewel, the city has a great high wall with twelve gates and twelve angels at the gates. The gates have written upon them the names of the twelve tribes of Israel, showing the ongoing significance in spite of sin and failure, of the Old Testament people of God.

The gates are to be found, three each in the east, west, north and south—all directions which shows totality—and the twelve foundations of the wall of the city have the names of the twelve apostles. This affirms again the importance, regardless of betrayal and imperfection, of those through whom God revealed himself (21:9-14).

The city is then measured, no doubt aiming to emphasize its perfection and completeness as the dwelling place of God. John now further describes the Holy city with extravagance and excess, attempting to capture its astonishing reality. It is made of pure gold, is transparent as glass, has walls of jasper, and the foundations that are visible are decorated with a list of precious stones. A vast array of dazzling colors and reflections abound. This picture of God's city is one of magnificence, beauty and brilliance, purity and assured rest (21:15-21).

Notice, there is no temple in the Holy city because God and the Lamb are its temple. This confirms that our direct community with them will be deeper, new and unlimited, far beyond that which was previously possible. Picture it as not less than what we already have, but superabundantly more. The city will not need sun or moon as God's glory will be its light and the Lamb its lamp. Light was there in the beginning and now will be total—always illuminating. We are to be plunged into and saturated with light as darkness disappears and is no more. There will be a universal knowledge of God as the nations follow God's light, but only those who belong to the Lamb may enter the city (21:22-27).

An angel shows John the river of life. The imagery of the water of life stands for the truth that life originates with God and the Lamb. In the midst of the city, life will burst forth and be present in all its fullness. The tree of life being full of fruit and leaves will bring healing for the nations. Healing will be a settled state in the age to come, not transitory or temporary as in the present age, and there will no longer be any curse. God's redeemed will have the joy and privilege of serving him.

Those who serve God, those who are redeemed, are said to see his face. This again affirms what we have seen previously. Community with God will be direct, not mediated. To see God face to face in the Old Testament meant death. Moses, in spite of his significant role in salvation history, was not allowed to see God's face. But now, those who belong to God, as signified by having his name on their foreheads, will see him face to face. What a gracious blessing.

The risen Lord announces he is coming soon. As Christians we are to be encouraged and to be living spirituality in expectancy, even though we don't know the day or hour of restoration. We are told to keep the words of the prophecy that John has been given. I think the thought here is that the church in every age is called to stand for Christ against Antichrist and to remain steadfast and loyal to him in the midst of pressures and persecution. God has faithfully revealed to us the end of history, and the consummation of his rule. His victory is sure, as is ours, on the basis of the blood of the Lamb. Therefore we are to worship God and him only (22:1-9).

The journey comes to a close with this awesome and inspiring revelation. Our ultimate destination is to have life together in everlasting community with God—the end of the journey and its beginning—living spirituality in a renewed, redeemed, and glorious heaven and earth.

Printed in the United States
120210LV00003BA/222/A